CW00530239

BRITAIN'S
HAUNTED
HERITAGE

BRITAIN'S HAUNTED HERITAGE

JOHN WEST

DB
PUBLISHING

Dedicated to Uri Geller, Stewart Evans, Jason Figgis, Julie Abbott and the staff at *Psychic News* magazine – fellow travellers

Acknowledgements

Thanks to Stewart Evans and Julie Abbott for providing photographs for this book. Thanks also to Rosie Evans for proofreading my original manuscript.

First published 2019 by DB Publishing, an imprint of JMD Media Ltd, Nottingham, United Kingdom.

Copyright © John West

All Rights Reserved. No part of this publication may be reproduced, stored in a retrieval system, or transmitted in any form, or by any means, electronic, mechanical, photocopying, recording or otherwise without the prior permission in writing of the copyright holders, nor be otherwise circulated in any form or binding or cover other than in which it is published and without a similar condition being imposed on the subsequent publisher.

ISBN 978-1-78091-603-3

Printed in the UK

CONTENTS

7   Introduction
     by Uri Geller

9   Foreword
     by Jason Figgis

12   In Search of Ghosts

Chapter One
13   The Naked Embrace

Chapter Two
27   The Gladwish Terror

Chapter Three
35   The Enigma of the Hexham Heads

Chapter Four
46   The Treasurer's House

Chapter Five
53   The Grey Man of Ben MacDhui

Chapter Six
63   The Curse of William Corder's Skull

Chapter Seven
75   Ghosts of the Bloody Tower

Chapter Eight
84   The Hairy Hands of Dartmoor

Chapter Nine
90   The Monks of St Dunstan's

Chapter Ten
100   The Green Lady of Fyvie Castle
and Other Haunting Tales

Chapter Eleven
107   Shadows of Evil

Chapter Twelve
119   The Crawling Lady of Ardachie

Chapter Thirteen
128   The Agony of Marie le Moyne

Chapter Fourteen
133   Ealing's House of Death

Chapter Fifteen
140   The Lady and the Butterfly

Chapter Sixteen
146   Beyond Harry Price -
The Ghosts of Borley Church

Chapter Seventeen
157   The Curse of the Setons

Chapter Eighteen
164   The Croglin Horror

Chapter Nineteen
174   The Beast of Merionethshire

Chapter Twenty
178   The Psychic legacy of Jack the Ripper

189   Recommended Reading

INTRODUCTION

by Uri Geller

With news in the press recently showing us the first images of the enigmatic phenomenon known as the black hole, seismic events both universal and terrestrial are fascinating people around the globe – perhaps more than ever before. Climate change and associated storms and other cataclysms are forcing people to look beyond their personal bubble into the world around them. People are searching for answers to existence and what the future might hold for the race we call – human.

(Jason Figgis)

Partly because of these recent events, the world of the paranormal is holding more fascination than perhaps any other period in human history. Ghost hunters abound, mediums are emerging from every strata of society and more and more manifestations of this 'other world' that runs in parallel to our own material world – are filling up the column inches, both in the printed word and digital domains.

The human mind is conflicted with what it knows to be real and what could possibly be manipulated through computer generated imagery. Nevertheless, the fascination grows.

They are calling films about haunted houses 'sleeper hits' because they are generating such revenues at the box office but these are not sleeper hits. These are films that speak to generations full of this fascination for all things outside their understanding of the material world and because of this, excellent books like this one you have just read, by excellent writers and inquisitive minds like John West, will continue to appear on the shelves of bookshops, both physical and digital.

Let us forever keep an open mind and continue to explore this wondrous planet that we call home and perhaps stare a little deeper into the day and the night, for what might linger on the periphery of our understanding – in order to understand it a little bit more.

Uri Geller
www.urigeller.com

FOREWORD

by Jason Figgis, Film Director

In the summer of 1978, as I was about to turn 12, I was part of a nocturnal scouting expedition to the notoriously haunted ruins of Lydican Castle in the tiny hamlet of Gort, Co Galway, in the scenic west of Ireland. As we gathered around the slowly fading embers of the campfire – set judiciously within the cavernous ruins – the boyish chat soon faded out as the troop succumbed to sleep.

(Bernadette Manton)

I felt as though I was beginning to dream when I sat bolt upright to the sound of footsteps ascending the weather-beaten stone spiral to the empty and windswept rooms above. What followed were angry voices raised in muffled altercation as weapons were drawn while spectral echoes of steel upon steel played out in the dark. A heavy door was slammed, its bolt drawn sharply into its mooring – then silence.

In the almost impenetrable gloom, other boys moved uneasily in their sleeping bags, but no one spoke. The silence was unbroken.

The exact sequence of eerie sounds repeated throughout the night at regular intervals and as the morning sun broke over the verdant horizon, we boys woke to ripples of conversation that tentatively addressed the experience of the night before.

So, it wasn't a dream. It turned out that we had all experienced the same phenomena. I could say that this event engendered my love of the supernatural and it would be a worthy place from where to continue the narrative but – although it cemented that love – the seed was sown by the BBC some six or seven years earlier on a cold Christmas Eve as I watched – pillow at the ready – the first instalment of Lawrence Gordon Clark's exemplary adaptations of Montague Rhodes James's seminal ghost stories for the seasonal offering *A Ghost Story for Christmas*.

From this thrilling moment love was born and I set about to acquire every book of ghost stories that I could get my hands on. Over the years I have collected first editions of James, Elliott O'Donnell and Lord Halifax, amongst others, and have visited and photographed almost every castle and mansion of the British Isles.

In 2002 I teamed up with the internationally acclaimed and celebrated photographer of the eerie, the late Sir Simon Marsden, as we embarked on a journey together across the length and breadth of Ireland – he was taking photographs for his new coffee table tome, *The Twilight Hour*, and I filming his every endeavour. The resulting book was a bestseller and the film (of the same name) – distributed by Discovery Channel to 150 countries – was festooned with excellent reviews, Irish Film and Television Award nominations and subsequently opened many doors with resulting opportunities and lasting friendships with like-minded people.

Several distributed documentaries, teen horror features and revenge dramas later and I found myself back in familiar territory at the immensely fogbound contours of the East Anglia coastline – specifically Aldeburgh in Suffolk. I was there to direct a feature documentary titled *The Haunting of M.R. James* – looking at the famed academic's influences – when I received a message from a journalist based in Suffolk, asking to interview me for the excellent magazine *Psychic News*.

It wasn't until I returned to Dublin that I was able to give full focus to the request and, over a series of phone conversations with John West, we soon discovered a huge amount in common. The interview questions were furnished and answered and we soon progressed to other things as a collaboration was born.

I was putting together the finishing touches to my Nikon-sponsored and Royal Photographic Society-patronised documentary feature *Simon Marsden: A Life in Pictures* when West professed a similar love of Marsden's oeuvre. We determined to work together to promote the film and it wasn't long before my new ally had secured interviews with several glossy magazines and numerous newspapers. We spoke daily but it wasn't until the BFI world premiere of the Marsden film some three months later, that we met in person. He conducted a Q&A with me post-premiere and we realised that we got on like the proverbial house on fire. Two days of meetings followed at London museums and quiet cafes, where we determined to cement our working relationship within a partnership called Figgis-West.

Nine weeks later we were on-set of our first film endeavour under this banner of an exciting (and appropriate) haunted house feature called *Winifred Meeks*. Having secured our leading lady in the form of multi award-winning actress Lara Belmont – who won worthy praise for her breakout performance as Ray Winstone's daughter in the harrowing feature film *The War Zone* (from tyro helmer Tim Roth) our small cast was cemented by talented newcomer Julie Abbott in the titular role of the troubled spirit.

At the time of writing, this film is in post-production and John West already has magazines and newspapers primed to cover its release. I was deeply honoured to be asked by John to write this foreword, as not only has he proven to be an excellent producer of film, but his extensive body of work as a journalist and historian never fails to impress me with its rhythm, energy, poetic grace and attention to thrilling detail. You can be assured that the following pages of this excellent book will hold your attention from early morning till late into the night, with a growing appetite for his work that will require regular attention.

Read on fellow travellers.

Jason Figgis
Dublin, Ireland, 2019
https://figgisjason.wixsite.com/director

IN SEARCH OF GHOSTS

It is said that Great Britain is the most haunted land on the planet with phantom grey ladies, ghostly cavaliers and spectral clergymen seemingly commonplace. Why this should be so is something that has been debated by scholars for decades. Has the mix of Celtic, Saxon, Viking and Norman blood made us more susceptible to the supernatural? Or, are the large number of Ley Lines to blame? Some believe that these lines of energy criss-cross our landscape and somehow greatly boost psychic activity in all those places where they intersect.

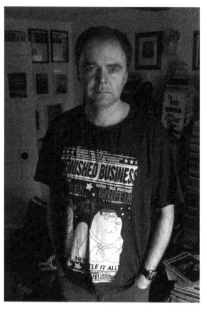

(Jason Figgis)

So what is a ghost? Some may be recordings generated by intense emotions that have imprinted themselves into the fabric of a building or even the ground. These images are then played back under certain atmospheric conditions or are activated by those who possess psychic abilities. Others may be the genuine souls of the dead, unable or unwilling to leave the earthly plane. And some, of course, may be simple hallucinations or even hoaxes.

Whatever your views on the paranormal, I hope that *Britain's Haunted Heritage* will provide you with a thrilling and informative look into our ghostly past, the result of over 35 years of personal study and investigation into the twilight world beyond death.

John West
Suffolk, 2019
www.johnwestmedia.com

Chapter 1

THE NAKED EMBRACE

I have always regarded the haunting of Langenhoe church one of the most pressive on record. A large and fascinating list of paranormal events were recorded there over a 22-year period – events that still baffle and confound even the most hardened sceptic to this very day.

Langenhoe village can be found a few miles south of Colchester in Essex. It is a bleak and lonely spot, rarely featuring on any tourist trail.

The church of St Mary the Virgin was largely 15th century, although parts did date back to the 11th century. It was badly damaged in the 'Great English Earthquake' of 1884 and was never structurally sound from then on.

Langenhoe Church after the earthquake. Some have suggested that the earthquake triggered the paranomal events that later occured within the church. (public domain)

In 1937 the Rev. Ernest A. Merryweather came to Langenhoe from a parish in the north of England. He had absolutely no interest in ghosts and had never experienced anything paranormal prior to becoming rector of the church.

Crucially, he kept a diary and it was not long before he began to fill it with detailed accounts of inexplicable phenomena encountered by him and others in the church and surrounding area. It all started with quite literally a bang!

I visited the church on 20 September 1937. It was a quiet autumn day. I was standing alone in the church, and the big west door was wide open. Suddenly it crashed to with such force that the whole building seemed to shake. Doors don't usually slam to as if an express train had hit them, when there is no palpable reason. This aroused my curiosity as to the cause.

The rector was certain that the wind could not have caused the door to close, nor did he believe it was a prank played upon him by a local.

Merryweather also encountered problems with his valise. This contained his books and vestments and was used by him when going to the church to conduct services.

On 5 November 1937, after the 11 o'clock service, I was about to leave the vestry and placed my robes in my valise. Having forgotten to put something else inside, I tried to open the catches for some time, then gave it up as hopeless; they were fixed tight. When I reached the bottom of the church lane, I tried again. The 'influence' had gone and the catches worked normally.

It should be noted that this was also witnessed by his friend.

Events now quietened down and it was not until 1945 that there was another strange occurrence. It was Easter Sunday and the rector, his housekeeper – a Mrs Gertrude Barnes – and her 13-year-old daughter, Irene, were in the church to decorate it with flowers. The housekeeper left a vase of flowers in a pew and went off to do something else. When she returned, the flowers had been taken from the vase and laid out on the

Langenhoe Church. (public domain)

pew. Both the rector and the daughter denied having moved the vase and no one else was in the church at the time of the incident.

Things again returned to normal but this was all to change one autumn day in 1947!

The rector was being shown round the local 18th-century hall – built on the site of earlier buildings – by a Mrs Cutting, the occupier. She led him to a front bedroom which was described by her as having 'something queer about it'. She admitted that she disliked it to such an extent that she refused to sleep there.

In a letter to A.C. Henning, rector of Borley – more of Borley later! – Merryweather described what happened next:

> *I was surprised at this, and said, 'but what a pleasant view you have out of the window.' Mrs Cutting went out of the room asking me to go and look at the other rooms, and then, as I turned round, I felt distinctly a woman's body against mine. One embrace, and the dear lady was off.*

He later admitted to Henning that the lady was naked!

In July 1948 the rector was celebrating Holy Communion. Suddenly, loud thudding noises were heard coming from the vestry. The sounds were described as being like several clods of earth being thrown at the door. These noises were also heard by the congregation. A search failed to find a likely cause. These noises were heard on nine more occasions that year, the last being in the month of December.

On 11 November, Merryweather left the church to get some coal from the churchyard in order to heat the church. Using an iron rod, he started to rake the coal. Suddenly, he felt a presence and upon impulse thrust the rod into the coal and placed his biretta on it. You can imagine his surprise as he witnessed it begin to revolve. He returned to the church – only to experience something even more shocking!

There had been problems with hooliganism in the area and the rector had took it upon himself to carry a dagger for protection. He was standing by the altar when the dagger was pulled from his belt and clattered to the floor. As this happened, he heard a woman say, *'You are a cruel man.'* The voice came from behind him but upon turning, no one was there.

December also proved eventful. The south door of the church dated from the 15th century but it had been blocked up after the earthquake of 1884. A figure of St George, a brass credence bell and two altar lights had been placed there. On 2 December, the rector heard what sounded like an old man's cough come from the statue. Moments later the credence bell rang. Again, a check of the church revealed no other person – living that is! – in the building. Several days later he heard what sounded like a rifle shot come from the figure of St George and upon inspection found piles of stained glass scattered in the chancel. The credence bell was heard to ring on several more occasions and this was also heard by the housekeeper and her daughter.

The year 1949 was to prove even more interesting. It was 21 August and the rector was holding Holy Communion. He suddenly noticed, near the west end of the church, the figure of a lady in a white-grey dress. She appeared to be about 30, was solid and was roughly five feet six inches in height. She was wearing a flowing head-dress which reached down to her shoulders. She appeared sad and walked with a slight stoop. She made no sound as she walked from near a window in the north wall, crossed the chancel and finally vanished at the corner of the south-west wall. The wall appeared to open up as the figure passed through, upon which it closed again. It later transpired that a door had once existed at the point where the figure vanished.

On 27 August, James Turner, a writer and broadcaster, visited the church along with his wife. They discovered that the latch of the vestry door had been yanked off and lay in two pieces on the ground. They were unable to open the door and assumed it was locked. Upon inserting the key it was discovered that the door was in fact unlocked and could now be opened. A large amount of plaster was found scattered across the floor. They climbed the tower and found two bricks on the top step. Both had been wrapped in newspaper. The paper was new and without dust and could only have been placed there recently. However, the rector was adamant that no one had been in the tower over the last few days. It was noted on that day the atmosphere in the church was extremely oppressive and frightening.

In January of the next year, Merryweather twice heard a female voice which appeared to say 'ow!' This occurred while he was measuring the south door of the church. Problems with the vestry door also persisted. On 3 June Mr William Ware, a former bell-ringer at the church, was there to replace some roof tiles. He tried to open the door, turning the key and lifting the latch. It refused to move. He went to a nearby cottage for help and upon returning, with a Mr Cross, found the door open.

Mr Ware then climbed a ladder to the roof, only to hear the church bell ring out twice. No one else was in the church. This was also heard by Mr Cross.

The phenomena persisted throughout the year. On 14 September, the rector smelt perfume in the church. The smell filled the whole building and appeared to be of spring violets.

On 28 September, music was heard. The rector was in the vestry when he heard the voice of a lady singing what sounded like plainsong chanting.

Langenhoe churchyard. (John West)

It appeared to come from the west end of the building. The chanting stopped suddenly and the sound of slow, heavy footsteps were heard walking up the nave. Merryweather quickly entered the main body of the church and the sound stopped. A search of the building again proved that he was alone. The music was also heard by two workmen a week later. The rector found them looking through the keyhole of the locked west door. He again heard the singing and thought it sounded French. The workmen refused to believe that the church was empty and so he told one of them to wait at the door while he entered the church through the east door. He asked the other man to go with him. They made their way through the church and unlocked the west door to let the other man in. A thorough search was then made of the whole building. It was empty. The workmen explained that they had been working at the hall, had heard the singing, and so entered the churchyard to investigate.

In December, the cupboard door in the vestry was found open on several occasions. It was always shut after a service, the church then being locked. Despite this, the cupboard continued to be found open. On one occasion, the rector's stole was found to have been wrapped around his vestments.

Another apparition was seen on Christmas Eve. The rector was alone and it was 10.15am. As he walked up the nave, towards the chancel, he saw a form glide in front of him. He got the impression of a man in modern clothing, possibly a tweed suit.

1951 saw yet more paranormal activity. On Sunday, 28 January the rector arrived at the church at approximately 10am. He removed some dead flowers and left the church for about 15 minutes. Upon his return, he noticed the impression of a white, chalky hand on the vestry door. He was certain that it had not been there before. Mrs Barnes and her daughter also saw it and thought it resembled a woman's hand. The impression lasted for ten days and then faded away.

The cupboard door opened on two separate occasions in March, but after that it never happened again.

On 17 June it was found that one of four candles has vanished from its holder after the morning service; a search failed to find it. During another service on 15 July, St Swithin's Day, a candle was seen by the whole congregation to go out as the saint's name was read. A loud spluttering and hissing was heard as if water had been thrown upon it. It should be noted that the roof did not leak. It was also dry and had not rained for several days.

On Saturday, 23 June the rector suddenly felt ill and experienced a malevolent presence in the churchyard. He felt he was being watched and felt that the presence wished him to leave. 'There was murder in the air,' he later said.

A sinister event also happened the following day. At the conclusion of a sermon, a lamp over the altar was seen to burst into flames. The lamp was also known to occasionally swing on its own.

And on Sunday, 8 July the female apparition again appeared during a service. Merryweather was at the end of a reading when he saw her in the aisle. She was dressed in the same clothing and was facing the statue of St George. She then floated through the statue and vanished through the blocked-up door. Only the rector witnessed this as the congregation was facing him and the apparition was behind them.

1951 ended with two further events. On 22 July the rector heard a loud pop right by his ear as he prepared for a service. He likened it to a cork pulled from a bottle. There was a wine bottle in the cupboard but it was unopened. On 9 September a candle went out for no apparent reason during a reading. This happened the next Sunday too, and some members of the congregation claimed to have heard a blowing sound as it went out. Draughts were ruled out and no one was near enough to the candle to physically blow it out.

1952 witnessed even more activity. On 8 June the rector experienced a terrible smell in the church. He later claimed it reminded him of a rotting corpse.

On Sunday, 5 August Merryweather heard hushed voices while in the vestry. They appeared to come from the chancel. Two or three people were having a heated conversation. One of the voices was most certainly male. No words could be made out and the conversation finally ended with a deep sigh. Again, a search of the church failed to reveal the people responsible.

Sunday, 12 October marked another appearance of a female apparition. It was approximately 10.45am and the rector was singing Psalm 119 before a service. He was at the point of the passage 'Rivers of water run down mine eyes, because they keep not thy law' when he suddenly felt that someone was standing near the lectern and looking at him. Looking across, he saw the figure of a young lady in a cream dress. She had blue eyes and her face was oval. He described her as having a 'strange, sad look'. She vanished, her dress being the last item to disappear.

The activity continued over the following years. The handle of a door was heard to rattle by Mrs Barnes. Upon opening it, no one was there. A lamp exploded, a door opened and closed on its own and footsteps were again heard by the rector.

Merryweather also said in a letter to the rector of Borley that on another occasion he saw the figure of a French cavalryman in the rectory grounds. He called out but was ignored. The man then vanished. This was also witnessed by a policeman. A search failed to locate the man.

In 1959 the Rev. Merryweather retired and the living of Langenhoe was combined with another parish. He died in 1965. St Mary's stood empty and neglected. It was finally demolished in 1962. The reason given was that the church was unsafe and too badly damaged to repair. Some claim that this was just an excuse and the demolition of the building was caused by a desire on the part of the church authorities to eradicate the ghosts. However, it should be noted that Merryweather had said that the church always seemed to be 'on the move' and was often in need of repair following the earthquake of 1884.

So what are we to make of this fascinating case? Some sceptics have argued that the rector made the whole thing up. Peter Underwood – the well-respected paranormal investigator – knew the rector and found him sensible, critical and 'often sceptical' regarding some of the stories connected with the hauntings. He was also open to a natural explanation for the activity in the church and impressed Mr Underwood as a very good witness. The rector also had nothing to gain and much to lose by talking about his story. Certain elements in the Church of England would have been less than pleased to hear him openly talk about ghosts haunting church property.

It should also not be forgotten that others also witnessed strange happenings in and around the church. Indeed, there were stories of ghosts in Langenhoe long before Merryweather became rector there. Locals spoke of a lady in white seen walking around the church and there was a story that the church bell rang when a rector died, sometimes for hours. Peter Underwood was also told by a Mrs Farthing that her aunt had warned her of a lady in black haunting the church. She was told this in 1910.

At least two cottages in the village were also said to be haunted, with reports being made of footsteps and varied poltergeist activity, including latches lifted and windows opened.

An interesting experience was also told to John Dening, a member of the Ghost Club, by a Mrs Booth. Her gypsy family often camped in a lane near the church and were all well aware of the reputation of the building. This would have been around 1908. Mrs Booth was 15 at the time and took her older sister one night to watch for ghosts. Just after midnight both heard the church bell ring twice. The younger sister then witnessed an apparition appear at the east end of the church. The figure was female and was dressed like a nun. It walked up the path and vanished through the north wall. The figure was heard to sing and appeared grey in the moonlight. The sister did not see the ghost but did hear the singing and also heard the rustling of the dress.

I am the first to admit that some of the activity heard by the rector and others could easily have had a natural explanation. As I have said before, the church was structurally unsound and some of the knocks, pops, bangs, the swinging lamp and sticking doors could be attributed to this. Vandalism was also a problem in the area and some of the damage to the church, such as the plaster on the floor and broken latch, could be blamed on hooligans. The same goes for the appearance of the bricks in the tower and perhaps also the gunshot.

However, that still leaves a vast and impressive list of ghostly activity which cannot easily be explained away. These include, apparitions, voices, singing and footsteps, not forgetting the naked embrace in the nearby hall!

So who or what was behind it all?

The Rev. Merryweather was told about a girl who allegedly had an affair with a former rector. She was supposedly murdered in the church when he tired of her. However, no names or dates are given and so this story must remain an interesting legend.

In 1958 seances were held in the church and at other locations. The medium was a Mrs Lampard and several messages were obtained which claimed to provide an alternative explanation for the hauntings. It was alleged that a Sir Robert Att Ford, supposedly Lord of the Manor in the reign of James I, was having an affair with a serving girl called Mary Brown. He stabbed her to death in the church following a heated argument. Her body was then hurriedly buried. However, none of this can be proved historically and so, like the other story of murder, must therefore remain sheer speculation.

And what of the more modern apparitions? What was behind the appearances of the man in a tweed suit and the French cavalryman in the rectory grounds? This case certainly throws up more questions than answers.

What is interesting to note is that Langenhoe can be directly linked to Borley – the same Borley made famous by Harry Price in the 1930s. The Waldegraves owned Borley and acquired Langenhoe manor through marriage in the 16th century. Several rectors in the 17th and 18th centuries held both livings and so would often travel between the two. The Rev. Merryweather certainly believed that the phantoms of Langenhoe and Borley were connected. He even thought that the lady who embraced him

Langenhoe churchyard. (John West)

was a member of the Waldegrave family and joked on one occasion that the non-appearance of the 'nun' in Langenhoe was down to her having flitted off to Borley for a visit. So was the 'nun' of Langenhoe the same figure – also a nun – witnessed in Borley? Sadly, we will never know.

It was said that Langenhoe was an unlucky place – perhaps even cursed. A member of the Waldegrave family was thought to have committed suicide in the hall. Other suicides were connected with the building and nine children, including the mother, also died there in the 19th century. The rectory was also a scene of a suicide. However, the mortality rate for children in the 19th century was high and suicides are not uncommon in rural areas. So one should not infer too much from this line of thought.

It is certain that Langenhoe church was very badly haunted. More than one entity was involved and the ghosts/spirits were not just confined to the church. This was also clearly more than a residual haunting/recording – recordings do not embrace you, pull a dagger from your belt and address you in a reprimanding tone!

Some believe that seismic activity can be linked to the appearance of ghosts and spirits. Did the earthquake of 1884 somehow trigger the hauntings? Like many explanations, it is just a theory, but an interesting one nonetheless. All we can safely say is that by 1908 the tradition of a ghostly lady haunting the area was already firmly established.

The Rev. Ernest Merryweather was clearly the crucial element in this story. That he witnessed so much has, as I said before, made some people cast doubt on his evidence. However, he was in the church far more often than any other person and so could naturally be expected to experience more.

I cannot also help thinking that maybe he had psychic abilities – on an unconscious level – and that the spirit of the lady was drawn to him. Was she perhaps seeking love and solace from the rector? If so, the story of the naked embrace is one of the most moving in the entire history of the paranormal.

We will never know the exact circumstances that contributed to this haunting, but it certainly remains one of the most puzzling and fascinating on record. One could go as far to say that Langenhoe church was once the most haunted buildings in Britain, the activity recorded there providing clear proof of life after death.

And what of Langenhoe today? The church has long gone but the graveyard can still be seen. The tombstones now stand lopsided and overgrown. The hall also remains.

And the ghosts? The churchyard still retains a sinister reputation – some visitors to the site report feeling drained of energy upon leaving there. So does a presence still linger on in this corner of the Essex countryside? Apparently so.

I have always hoped that one day a medium will travel to Langenhoe and release whatever remains there. After so many centuries, I would like to think that the spirits there will finally find some peace in the hereafter.

Chapter 2

THE GLADWISH TERROR

Hauntings can take many forms. Some can best be described as a recording – a fleeting shadow of a life long extinguished. Others, however, cannot be explained away in such simple terms and still defy explanation to this very day. For example, can a tormented soul's anger and torment forever bind it to this world? The 1930s case of Robert Thurston Hopkins and his encounter in Gladwish Wood is one such example – a haunting that I still regard as one of the most terrifying on record.

Rudyard Kipling once described the Sussex Downs as 'haunted landscapes' and had a theory that certain areas exuded a benevolent or maleficent influence on those who came into contact with them. Gladwish Wood (then also known as Glidwish Wood), near Burwash in Sussex, was one such spot. He regarded the ancient woodland as a foreboding place: 'There is a wood about a mile from my house which is full of a sense of ancient ferocity and evil. I have sometimes, while taking an evening walk through it, felt a secretive and menacing feeling all around me, holding me expectant and always on guard. Yes, and in this evil wood everything is evil. The paths around it are alive with adders; the roots of the trees seem to have been contorted by the Devil; and are always waiting to trip one up – the clinging, trailing brambles reach out to tear at one's eyes with a horrible suggestion of intelligence.'

He even claimed to have had an encounter there with 'a spirit of some kind … a very unpolite fellow he is too, for one evening something suddenly gripped me and despite my attempts to walk forward I was gradually forced back. I felt some unseen, unknown power just pushing against me, and in the end I was compelled to turn around and leave the wood in a most undignified manner – just as if someone was ejecting me with the command "Now then—out you go".'

Kipling spoke of his experiences to Robert Thurston Hopkins, president of the Society of Sussex Downsmen. Hopkins was a man with a deep interest in the paranormal and in the 1930s had even organised ghost walks in the south of England. Such was the popularity of these events that the press would often send representatives to report on any ghostly forms encountered.

Hopkins was fascinated by Kipling's encounter in Gladwish Wood and decided to organise an investigation. He found 30 people willing to join him, including a friend and journalist by the name of Blunden.

The group arrived in the village of Burwash at approximately 11.30pm and soon found themselves facing the moonlit wood. Those present were all struck by the menacing appearance of the place and one, a local, explained that no one from Burwash would enter the wood at night because of the weird sounds often heard there. These included, moans, grunts and footsteps. It was also rumoured that a body had once been hidden in the area.

Blunden was intrigued by all this and asked Hopkins if he could visit the wood alone. Hopkins tried to dissuade him as he was not keen to see the party split up. He was also worried that his friend may hurt himself as the wood was full of pools and old medieval pits. Blunden, however, was in no mood to listen:

'I can't say I believe in ghosts', he said. 'But on the other hand nor do I disbelieve in them … anyway, I mean to go into the wood and have a look around.'

Hopkins reluctantly agreed but explained that he would not be taking the others into the trees for fear of them getting lost.

Blunden said that he would cross the wood and asked the others to walk along the edge and meet him on the other side. He agreed to blow a police whistle at regular intervals so that the group would know where he was. He also asked Hopkins to blow his own whistle so that he would know where they were.

Rudyard Kipling wrote of his sense of evil after entering Gladwish Wood. (pubic domain)

Blunden entered the wood and was soon lost to sight. They could hear him crashing through the ferns, fallen branches and brambles that littered the wood. A whistle was heard and Hopkins blew his in reply. At this point, the group decided to stop for some refreshments and continued to listen for Blunden while they did so.

Twenty minutes passed and not a sound could be heard from the forbidding trees. Hopkins, now slightly concerned, decided to continue around the edge of the wood in the hope that Blunden was waiting on the other side.

As they moved off, Hopkins saw that another of his party, Blandish, was standing motionless beside a gap in the hedge bordering the wood. He explained to Hopkins that he had heard footsteps and it seemed that someone was following the trail left by Blunden.

Hopkins called on the party to remain quiet and they listened. He too heard the footsteps and even thought, along with two others, that he could see a dark figure moving through the ferns.

Hopkins blew his whistle but Blunden still failed to answer. Suddenly, and without warning, the group heard a long drawn out moan of despair echo across the woods. Hopkins, worried that Blunden had injured himself, asked a Dr Salmond to take charge of the party and rushed into the wood with Blandish to see what had happened.

They were both hampered by the undergrowth, mud and ponds but finally came across Blunden in what appeared to be the middle of the wood. They were shocked to discover him making strange choking noises, seemingly oblivious to their presence. He finally recognised them and admitted to meeting 'something' in the trees.

Blunden explained that after leaving the group, he had forced a path through the trees and after a quarter of a mile had found a track that appeared to lead through the centre of the wood. The trees were illuminated by the moon and so he was able to easily follow the track as it twisted through the undergrowth. He came across a few nocturnal animals, including owls, and became accustomed to the various noises they produced when suddenly he heard the sounds of moaning and choking. He realised the noises were getting closer and noticed that a large and dark shape was moving swiftly towards him. He suddenly felt an overwhelming sense of sadness and doom and quickly decided to move along the path in the hope that it would bring him out of the wood and away from whatever was approaching him. At one point, he left the path but became disoriented and realised that he had walked in a circle and was actually back where he had first heard the moans. He stopped and listened and realised that a man was moving towards him from out of the darkness ... what he saw next was something that would haunt him to his dying day.

A form burst forth from the undergrowth and staggered towards him. It was the shape of a man coughing and choking as he moved, all the time clutching his throat with both hands. As he got nearer, Blunden was terrified to see the flesh around the bulging eyes was rotten. The long neck was withered and the head appeared to bob and nod, 'like the head of a daffodil shaken by the wind.' Blunden instinctively knew that the man had been hanged and had been dead for many, many years.

Despite this, the journalist thought for a moment that he was the victim of a hoax and even suspected that one of his fellow walkers was behind it. With this in his mind, he rushed at the man with his walking stick. The figure stopped as he did this and seemed to be aware of him for the very first time. Blunden was now within arms-length of the figure and struck it on the head. He was shocked to see the skull-like head immediately smash into pieces of bone, the fragments of which fell upon the leaf covered floor.

Upon witnessing this, Blunden fled the scene and appeared to lose all reason. He remembered nothing else until he was found by his friends. Hopkins was convinced that Blunden was telling the truth and so decided – some say foolishly – to return to the wood to see if he could solve the mystery.

A month later, Hopkins found himself back in a moonlit Gladwish Wood. He was accompanied again by Blandish and both were armed with torches and stout walking sticks. They decided to retrace Blunden's original route in order to replicate the events from a month before.

They had been walking for about half an hour when both thought they heard a moan in the distance. Whatever was making the sounds was apparently heading towards them, crashing through the undergrowth in a seemingly desperate attempt to reach them. Hopkins and Blandish decided to hide behind a fallen tree and waited, not without some apprehension, to see what would emerge from the undergrowth.

Within seconds a man burst through the trees and together they both shone their torches upon the figure. It was exactly as Blunden described. Hopkins later swore that he would never forget the horrific sight of the man's almost fleshless face, eyes bulging and the long neck hanging to one side. The figure uttered choking sounds but fortunately seemed unaware of their presence. It staggered past them and disappeared into the night, the sounds of groaning and choking gradually fading away until they could hear it no more.

It was hardly surprising that Hopkins and Blandish vowed never again to return to the haunted wood. Both, however, were still determined to discover the history of the place and began researching local records in an effort to find anything that could account for the apparition. After extensive research, they finally discovered something that could have a bearing on the case.

In 1828 a poacher called Benjamin Russell lived in the area with his wife Hannah. Their marriage was far from happy and Hannah had a considerable reputation due to her violent temper, including threats made to her husband. They had a young lodger, David Leany, who was a labourer and not averse himself to poaching when the opportunity arose.

One night, Benjamin told his wife that both he and Leany were going to steal some sacks of corn from a local farm. Hannah was violently against the plan but was ignored.

The theft went ahead and both men made for home with the stolen corn. It was near Gladwish Wood that Benjamin tripped and fell heavily, the sack falling to the ground as he rolled away from it. Leany rushed to help but was horrified to discover that his friend had died. He rushed home to Hannah and told her what had happened. Both decided to hide

Benjamin's body, fearful that the theft of the corn would be linked to them – a convicted thief could face execution in the 1820s. The body was hidden in Gladwish Wood and the corn disposed of.

The next day Leany called on the local police and told them that Russell had fallen down dead in the wood. He explained that he had hidden the body under brambles until it could be removed by the authorities.

At the inquest, evidence was given by a Dr Evans who stated that Russell had actually died of arsenic poisoning. It was also noted that Hannah had threatened her husband on several occasions. Gossip also claimed that Hannah and Leany were lovers and had everything to gain by seeing the husband dead.

A trial was held at Lewes Assizes in July 1828 and Dr Evans again stated his conviction that Russell had died from ingesting 60 grains of arsenic in his food. Gideon Mantell, a doctor and geologist, was also present in the court but rejected the poisoning theory. He explained that Russell had clearly died of a heart attack. His argument carried much weight but events soon conspired against the accused when Mantell was called out of court to attend a seriously ill patient. Upon his return he found that both prisoners had been found guilty and sentenced to death.

Mantell was determined to prove their innocence and continued to raise objections to the verdict. However, the court's verdict was upheld and Leany was hanged.

Leany continued to maintain his innocence until the very end, telling the prison chaplain that, 'I beg of you to believe me when I say I am innocent and to prove it I shall return to haunt the people who have hounded me to my death.'

Hannah Russell also faced the hangman's rope but her execution was postponed due to a technical objection to her sentence. Dr Mantell used this time in order to gather more evidence, including consulting other medical men who agreed that the verdict and medical evidence were unsound. Dr Evans was finally forced to admit that he had exaggerated the amount of arsenic in the body and conceded that Benjamin Russell had probably died of a heart attack.

Hannah was released and the authorities reluctantly acknowledged that Leany had been executed for a crime that he did not commit.

So did Leany really return after death? Hopkins certainly was convinced that he had. He was prepared to admit that one person could become confused and imagine a ghost in the wood but refused to believe that three different people could all have the same hallucination.

The ghost of David Leany is still said to haunt the ancient woodland. One can only hope that he will eventually find peace.

Hopkins died in 1958, his reputation as an author established with numerous books on ghosts and literary figures such as H. G. Wells and Oscar Wilde.

And what of Rudyard Kipling, the man who first brought the case to Hopkin's attention? He died in 1936 and is now said to haunt his old home, Bateman's, which lies near Gladwish Wood.

Chapter 3

THE ENIGMA OF THE HEXHAM HEADS

Two ancient-looking stone heads are unearthed in a Northumbrian town. An academic is asked to study them and suddenly finds herself terrorised by a creature that appears to be half-man and half-wolf. The heads then vanish under mysterious circumstances and are never seen again.

Would it surprise you to learn that the events I have just described are based on fact? So are there such things as werewolves? Read on and decide for yourself.

It was late May/early June in 1971 when two boys, Colin and Leslie Robson, unearthed a curious looking pair of heads in the garden of their home at 3 Rede Avenue in Hexham, Northumberland. Colin was 11 years of age, his brother two years younger.

Both objects were roughly 6cm high and appeared to be made of a grey-greenish stone. They were later dubbed 'the boy' and 'the girl' by researchers of the case. The 'boy' had hair which was modelled in stripes. The 'girl', or the 'hag' as she later became known, possessed a beak-like nose and eyes that were described as 'wildly-bulging'. It may have been a coincidence but Colin had made a small pottery head for a school competition shortly before finding the heads in the garden. It bore a slight resemblance to the stone heads and Colin had said that the idea of making it had just come to him. From what later occurred, can we assume that he had been influenced by the heads even before their discovery?

It soon became apparent that there was something distinctly sinister and unworldly about these two seemingly harmless stone objects. The heads were placed on a shelf in the house but were found to have moved to face the spot from where they had been unearthed. Poltergeist activity was also noted. Much of this seemed to take place around 2.30 in the morning. Glass was found shattered on a daughter's bed, doors opened, lights were turned on and off, pictures fell off walls, bottles exploded or moved and a mirror was found lying unbroken in a frying pan. A flower was later seen to bloom in the spot where the heads had been found. The ground above the find spot also glowed with an eerie light.

The Robson's neighbours at 1 Rede Avenue also had a terrifying experience. The mother, Mrs Nellie Dodd, was staying up to care for an ill daughter. Her ten-year-old son Brian had said that something was touching him and pulling his hair. The dog was also scared. The mother dismissed Brian's complaints as imagination but then saw a shape move towards her. It touched her leg and then left the bedroom, padding down the stairs as if on its hind legs. She later described it as being half human and half sheep-like – the upper half being that of an animal. The feet were described as being cloven. The mother went downstairs and found the front door wide open.

Prior to this event, Mrs Dodd's children had said there was a 'horrible' feeling in the house. The sounds of an animal pattering across a floor had also been heard. Mrs Dodd and her family were later rehoused.

It was later claimed that a theft from a nearby abattoir was behind the apparition. A man had apparently stolen a sheep from the building and had carried it down Rede Avenue on the night in question. Sceptics have claimed that a sleepy Mrs Dodd simply noticed the thief through her window and mistook the man and the carcass for a monster. However, this story only emerged many years later and does not take into account that the events all occurred *inside* the house. It is also interesting to note that there were stories about the abattoir being haunted by a similar apparition to the one seen by Mrs Dodd.

It was decided to send the heads to the Museum of Antiquities in Newcastle for further examination. They, in turn, sent them to a Dr Anne Ross, an expert on ancient Celtic stone heads. She concluded that they

16th-century woodcut of a werewolf (public domain)

were roughly 1,800 years old and were probably connected to a Romano-British shrine which may have stood in the area – the head was believed by the Celts to be the home of the soul and was also highly prized as a trophy in battle.

Dr Ross later described what happened in her Southampton home after she took possession of the artefacts:

Though there was nothing unpleasant about the appearance of the heads, I took an immediate, instinctive dislike to them. I left them in the box they had been sent in, and put it in my study. I planned to have them geologically analysed, and then to return them as soon as possible to the North.

A night or two after they arrived – I didn't connect this experience with the heads until later – I woke suddenly at about 2am, deeply frightened and very cold. I looked towards the door, and by the corridor light glimpsed a tall figure slipping out of the room. My impression was that the figure was dark like a shadow, and that it was part animal and part man. I felt compelled to follow it, as if by some irresistible force.

I heard it, whatever it was, going downstairs, and then I saw it again, moving along the corridor that leads to the kitchen: but now I was too terrified to go on. I went back upstairs to the bedroom and woke Dick, my husband. He searched the house and found nothing – no sign at all of the disturbance. We thought that I must have had a nightmare (though I could hardly believe that a nightmare could seem so real) and decided to say nothing about it.

A few days later, when the house was empty, my teenage daughter Bernice came home at about 4pm, about two hours before Dick and I returned from London. When we arrived home, she was deathly pale and clearly in a state of shock. She said that something horrible had happened, but at first would not tell us what. But eventually the story came out.

When she had come in from school, the first thing she had seen was something huge, dark and inhuman on the stairs. It had rushed towards her, vaulted over the bannisters, and landed in the corridor with a soft thud which made her think its feet were padded like those of an animal.

It had run towards her room, and, though terrified, she felt that she
had to follow it. At the door, it had vanished, leaving her in the state
in which we found her.

We calmed her down as best we could, and feeling puzzled and
disturbed ourselves, searched the house. Again, there was no sign of any
intruder – nor did we expect to find any.

Dr Ross said the figure was covered in black hair and was roughly six feet tall – the upper half being that of a wolf, the lower half being that of a man. She went on to say how she had often felt a cold presence in the house and had more than once heard the same soft thud of an animal's pads near the stairs. This once happened when the family were having dinner in the dining room. A search failed to find anything to account for the sounds but it was noted that the hall was freezing. Dr Ross's study door was also seen to burst open and the family cats were noticed to freeze, hackles up, staring at some unseen presence. Visitors to the house commented on a sense of evil and her husband, although never witnessing the creature, also heard and felt its presence. On one occasion, he had been ill in bed when he suddenly heard a loud crash and the soft thud of something jumping over the stairs. This was also heard by the daughter. The son also witnessed the creature on one occasion. He described it as being black in colour, having glowing red eyes and pointed ears. He also recalled that the drop from the bannisters to the floor was roughly 25 to 30 feet and that no living creature could have jumped that far without injuring itself.

It should be stressed at this point that Dr Ross had not heard about the figure seen in the Dodd's home. Nor had she been made aware of the other events connected with the heads prior to her taking possession of them.

Dr Ross finally decided to remove the heads, including several others, and had the building exorcised by a priest, who said that the heads were drawing power from one another. A spiritualist friend also warned her to dispose of them, claiming that she would certainly die if she kept them.

The heads were later seen by a scientist friend who refused to have anything to do with them. He said that such heads often seemed to be associated with car accidents he had experienced in the past. He also said that he did not like the look of them. Eventually, they found themselves in the hands of a Dr Robins, an inorganic chemist, who was investigating a theory that minerals could store sounds and images, replaying them back like a video player under the right conditions – this idea later becoming widely known as the 'Stone Tape theory'. Interestingly, it was found that both heads contained large amounts of quartz.

Dr Robins never saw the entity witnessed by Dr Ross or Mrs Dodd. However, he did experience other strange activity. When he first put the heads in his car to take them home, he found that all the dashboard electrics had gone dead.

He soon began to believe that the 'girl' head was the centre of the trouble. He found 'her' disquieting and started to feel very uncomfortable when the heads were facing him. He decide to turn them round but got the distinct impression that, as he did so, the girl's eyes 'slid round' to watch him.

Once, as he left his house, he told the heads, 'Let's see something when I get back!' He quickly returned to collect a book and found the atmosphere in the house 'almost electric with a stifling, breathless quality.' He attributed this to the head of the 'girl'.

The heads were then taken to Frank Hyde, an engineer with an interest in dowsing. Tests were carried out using dowsing rods and a pendulum. Both reacted violently when held near the 'girl'. The 'boy' produced no results. Both heads were then enclosed in a copper-wire cage which Hyde claimed had somehow diminished the activity within them.

It is at this point in the narrative that I must introduce Desmond Craigie to the reader. Mr Craigie, a former occupant of the house where the heads had been unearthed, claimed in 1972 that he had made them for his daughter in 1956! He further stated that the heads were not carved but were moulded using materials from a factory which made concrete posts. He had made three heads in all but one was damaged and thrown away. The other two were later lost in the garden. However, Dr Ross was unimpressed with this revelation and repeated her belief that the heads were from the Romano-British period. She also said that tests had shown the heads were not moulded.

An analysis by Frank Hodson, Professor of Geology at Southampton University, confirmed this. He said that the heads had been carved and could be made of sandstone from the Hexham area. He also believed that they could have originally been covered in lime plaster.

But another academic disagreed with his findings. Dr Robson, senior lecturer in geology at Newcastle University, also examined the heads and concluded that they were actually made of moulded cement.

So who was correct? It does appear that Dr Robson was in error when he dismissed the heads as being moulded from modern materials. It was later revealed by Prof Hodson that both heads had contained absolutely no traces of calcium silicate. Calcium silicate is the major component of cement, so the heads could never have been made in the way suggested by either Mr Craigie or Dr Robson. The heads were also described as being very dense. This would also rule out materials such as crushed limestone or marble being used in their manufacture.

Dr Ross later asked Mr Craigie to make further heads in order for her to compare them to the originals. He agreed to this but she found that his attempts to make new versions of the heads were very unlike the original pair.

So what are we to make of this mystery? Sceptics have dismissed the whole case as nonsense, happily citing the claim that Mr Craigie made the heads for his daughter. But was he really telling the truth? Could he have made the statement in order to gain notoriety for himself? It later emerged that Mr Craigie had a reputation as an attention seeker, joker and hoaxer. On one occasion, he even dressed up as a tramp to fool his neighbours. He certainly gained a tremendous amount of publicity after declaring that he had made the heads. And at least one person connected with the case has suggested that he may have had a financial motivation. The claims made by Mr Craigie must be treated with extreme caution and, in my opinion, be dismissed for the reasons cited above.

And what of Dr Anne Ross? She was a noted scholar, author and historian – a person with an outstanding track record in the field of Celtic studies. She certainly had no reason to fabricate the story about seeing a werewolf-like creature in her home. She must also be applauded for having the courage to go public with her experiences. Many readers would surely agree that she had much to lose by doing so. Confess a belief in the paranormal and you will find many a career irreparably damaged thanks to the hostility and mockery of the sceptics. I know of several academics and politicians, one of whom is now a household name, who firmly believe in the afterlife and reincarnation. However, none would ever dream of going public with their beliefs for fear of mockery.

We must also remember that members of Dr Ross's family had also seen or heard the creature. And what of the human/sheep-like apparition seen by Mrs Dodd? Was it really a man carrying a sheep as some have claimed? And let us also not forget the strange events witnessed by the Robson family before the heads were sent to Dr Ross. Finally, Dr Robins also experienced unusual activity when in possession of the heads. All of these people could not have been lying. It is quite apparent that something of a paranormal nature was happening and it was directly connected to the artefacts.

I have already mentioned that both heads contained quartz. So did they act as a storage battery for some form of negative energy?

What of the 'werewolf' itself? Could it have been an 'elemental', a spirit that derives reality from the human mind? This may sound far-fetched but writers such as Elliott O'Donnell had no doubt as to the reality of such entities. O'Donnell also believed that these beings attached themselves to ancient burial sites and were often malignant. It may interest the reader to learn that a local Hexham tradition points to Rede Avenue standing on the site of an ancient burial ground.

An elemental was said to be a mixture of both human and animal. O'Donnell himself claimed to have often witnessed them and was certain that they could by generated by vicious thoughts and actions. Colin Wilson also believed that they could be created by the human mind. In his book *Mysteries*, he describes how Alexandra David-Neel (see her book *Magic and Mystery in Tibet*) managed to create a phantom monk which appeared so solid that it was mistaken as a real person by a herdsman. She soon began to lose control of her creation, the monk becoming increasingly hostile and malignant. It took her six months of concentrated effort to 'de-materialise' it. Wilson also mentions a book, *Psychic Self-Defence*, in which the author, Dion Fortune, tells how she accidentally created an elemental in the shape of a wolf. It soon began to terrorise the household until she finally managed to re-absorb it.

So what if the Hexham heads were really Romano-British in origin? Was the entity simply a manifestation of a god or spirit worshipped there? Dr Ross believed that Rede Avenue may have stood on the site of a shrine. The image of the wolf certainly played a key role in Celtic life and belief. Indeed, Celtic reverence and fear of the wolf can be found throughout Western Europe and Great Britain. The Romans also embraced native religions and would erect temples and shrines to suitably romanised local gods and goddesses after conquering a region. For instance, the Gallo-Roman god Silvanus, often depicted wearing a wolf skin, has been linked by some scholars to a Celtic wolf totem-god of the dead.

So was the creature created by the emotions and thoughts of the priests and worshippers? And were these images and emotions then accidentally recorded by the quartz in the heads, only to be replayed under certain conditions? It is only a theory but one that may provide at least a partial explanation for some of the phenomena.

However, the heads simply acting as a crude video projector would not account for all the things reported in this case. What of the poltergeist-like activity, the boy who had his hair pulled and the apparent interaction between Dr Robbins and the 'female' head? Why were Dr Ross and her daughter compelled to follow the creature rather than run away in the opposite direction as you would expect? Many aspects of this case would suggest that the elemental was more than just a mindless projection from our remote past. Did it take on a life of its own, like Alexandra David-Neal's monk or Dion Fortune's wolf?

And why did Mrs Dodd see a figure that resembled a sheep rather than the werewolf-like creature seen by Dr Ross? Mrs Dodd did live near a building supposedly haunted by a man with a sheep's head. Had she heard of this tale prior to her own experience? Dr Ross admitted to being psychic, her mother also possessing the same ability. Crucially, the academic had also confessed to an interest in wolves as a child and admitted that she had seen phantom wolves in her youth. So was the entity able to tap into the minds of the witnesses, using their subconscious thoughts and fears to manifest itself? This could explain why it appeared in different guises to different witnesses.

Sadly, many of those associated with this case are now dead. Dr Ross tragically developed dementia and later could not even remember her career as an academic. Her husband and step-daughter also passed away. Mrs Robson, Mrs Dodd and Mr Craigie are also dead. However, the surviving children of Dr Ross, Mrs Robson and Mrs Dodd still insist that the paranormal events witnessed by their parents and themselves did take place. And let us not forget that Dr Ross never once doubted her conviction that the heads were at the root of the problems experienced by her and others.

Rede Avenue is still occasionally visited by those interested in the case. It was never confirmed if the houses were built on a Romano-British shrine or burial ground. Poltergeist activity is still said to occur in some of the homes.

So what finally happened to the heads? Peter Underwood, the well-known author of books on the supernatural, was told that they had been reburied on two separate occasions. However, strange events were reported in the areas where they were hidden and they were quickly dug up again. He was unable to discover what had happened to them after that.

All we can say for certain is that they were never seen again after being sent to Frank Hyde. He was later badly injured in a car accident and has since proved untraceable.

I have been told by one informant that both heads were destroyed during a further 'scientific' examination. Another, claims that they are now hidden in the basement of a museum alongside other 'troublesome' artefacts. Yet another source states with conviction that the heads are now in the possession of a private collector who refuses to identify himself for fear that he will be forced to return the heads to the Robson family.

Chapter 4

THE TREASURER'S HOUSE

'I don't know about ghosts – you know, I had never seen a ghost before that day, and I've never seen one since. But I do know what I saw that day in the cellar.'
Harry Martindale

York is one of the jewels in Britain's crown. It can boast over 2,000 years of history and also claims to be the most haunted city in Britain, if not the world. Indeed, it can boast probably the most fascinating ghost story in the whole history of paranormal research – the Roman soldiers of Eboracum!

York was originally founded by the Roman army some 30 years after the Roman invasion of Britain in 43AD. A legionary fortress, known as Eboracum, was sited on the flat ground above the River Ouse – the area later occupied by the Minster and surrounding medieval buildings and streets. The first legion to occupy the site was the Ninth, consisting of some 5,500 men. They mysteriously vanished from the army rolls in the second century and were replaced by the Sixth Legion. The Sixth remained in York for the rest of the Roman occupation, disappearing from history in the fourth century when the last regular troops were withdrawn from Britain to defend the now crumbling empire.

After the fall of Rome, York's Roman monuments gradually vanished under the successive buildings of York's later inhabitants. One of these is known as the Treasurer's House.

The Treasurer's House originally dates from the medieval period and was used as the home for the treasurer of the nearby Minster. It served in

A stretch of York's Roman and Medieval defences. (John West)

this capacity until 1547 when it passed into the hands of several private owners. The house was finally given to the National Trust in the 1930s and has remained in their care ever since.

In February 1953 it was decided to install a new central heating system in the cellar of the building. A local plumbing firm was used and Harry Martindale, an 18-year-old apprentice, was sent there to carry out the work. He found himself working alone in the cellar, using a single light which he fixed to the ceiling. He decided to stand his ladder in a six-foot trench which Harry noted had been excavated to a depth of roughly 18 inches – the cellar was roughly 18 feet square. Unbeknown to Harry, his ladder was resting on one of the Roman roads – the Via Decumana – which had led from one of the fortress gates to the headquarters building which stood on the site of the present Minster.

Nothing eventful happened on the first day but on the second day events proved rather more dramatic. It was about lunch time and Harry

Treasurer's House. (public domain)

was standing on the third or fourth rung of the ladder, knocking holes in the cellar ceiling with a hammer and chisel. He suddenly heard what he later described as 'just a blare of a note' which kept getting louder and seemed to come from the very wall itself. He assumed that it was a radio but this conviction quickly changed when he suddenly saw the plumed helmet of a man holding a long, battered, trumpet-like instrument appear from the very wall beneath him! The figure was roughly at Harry's waist height and to his right. It was hardly surprising that upon seeing the figure, Harry fell back from the ladder, scrambling in terror into the corner of the cellar.

The soldier emerged from the wall but was only visible from the knees up until he came to an exposed section of Roman road, upon which his whole figure could be seen. The ghost came at a slight angle to Harry and continued walking towards the far wall. But that was not all. A man on horseback now also appeared behind the first soldier. The horse appeared more like a carthorse than a stallion, indeed Harry was struck by the horse's bushy fetlocks as it crossed the trench and Roman road.

The horseman was then quickly followed by approximately 20 soldiers, all marching in pairs. None of the figures appeared to notice the crouching figure of the terrified plumber in the cellar corner.

The first thing that struck Harry was how small the soldiers were – about five feet in height. He was also surprised that the figures looked nothing like he imagined ghosts to be – misty and see-through – the sort you could find in a good many novels and films of the time. Indeed, these figures were completely solid and appeared living. He noticed that they were unshaven and weary, more like a rabble than the disciplined troops of popular imagination. The helmets came under the chin and each had a plume which came down the back of their heads. The tunics appeared to be of leather while the skirts were green with strips of leather attached. Each had leather sandals with straps and these were tied up from their ankles to their knees. The soldiers also carried a short sword or oversized dagger on their right side. Some also carried spears and held round shields with featured a large boss in the middle. None of the soldiers spoke clearly but Harry could hear a distinct mumbling emanating from them as they walked across the cellar. The sound of the horse's hooves could also be heard.

After the last of the soldiers vanished into the far wall, Harry scrambled out of the cellar, leaving his ladder and all his tools behind. He found the curator of the building, who, noting his shocked state, said, 'By the look of you, you've seen the Roman soldiers!'

Unbeknown to Harry, the house had a tradition of hauntings connected with the Romans. In the 1920s, when the house was in private hands, a fancy dress party was held there. One guest was amused to find herself facing a Roman soldier who barred her way to the cellar with a spear as she attempted to walk by him. She assumed someone was playing a practical joke on her but a search of the house revealed no one had come dressed as a Roman.

Harry left the house and quickly returned to his employer in Micklegate, not far from the house. He told him in no uncertain terms what he could do with his job before calling on his doctor. The doctor noted his patient's shocked appearance and duly signed him off for two weeks. These medical records were later produced by the doctor as proof of Harry's experience on that February day.

Harry later joined the Minster police force and only publicly spoke about his experience in the early 1970s after some of his friends leaked to the press what he had seen. Since then, it has become one of the most famous ghost stories in the world.

So what are we to make of Harry's sighting? For me, the description of the soldiers is crucial evidence. In the 1950s the widely accepted image of a Roman soldier bore no resemblance to the description as given by Harry. Indeed, look at any book or film from the 50s and you will find Roman soldiers depicted as clean shaven, tall, square jawed, complete with red, spotless uniforms and rectangular shields.

Harry was later interviewed in the 1970s by archaeologists who tried to get him to change his story as to how the soldiers looked. They said the swords were not carried on the right side. They also stated that the leather straps on the soldier's feet could never have gone up to the knees. This was against all accepted historical evidence. To his credit, Harry stuck to his story, never wavering in his conviction that he had seen Roman soldiers on that February day back in 1953.

It later emerged that Harry had been right all along. Archaeological evidence and academic opinion later confirmed that Roman soldiers of the late Roman empire did indeed look exactly as Harry described.

Another theory is that the figures were auxiliaries – non-Roman troops – drafted into the fortress garrison for special duties and so could possibly date from an earlier period. Auxiliary uniforms differed from standard legionary equipment, including oval or round shields rather than the usual rectangular ones. Some have further speculated that these auxiliaries formed part of the Ninth Legion which disappeared under mysterious circumstances sometime in the second century.

Treasurer's House. (public domain)

So how could an 18-year-old apprentice plumber, with no interest in history, have known something that even the experts of the day were unaware of? We can only conclude that he did indeed witness Roman soldiers some 1,500 years after the Roman Empire abandoned Britain.

So were the soldiers there in spirit or were they a recording, somehow triggered by the activity in the cellar? The fact that they did not notice the plumber's presence, even though he was just a few feet away, suggests that they were recordings and not conscious entities.

Some paranormal investigators believe that intense human emotions, such as fear or anger, can be recorded into the fabric of a building or even the soil. Under the right conditions, these events can be played back like a DVD or video tape. It should be noted that the soldiers were described as weary and ill-looking. Had they returned from a terrible battle or were they perhaps Eboracum's last patrol, leaving their fortress home in the fourth century to face an uncertain future on the continent? If so, no wonder their emotions lingered on down the centuries.

So what of the cellar today? It is now open to the public and you can visit the actual spot where Harry saw the ghosts.

So do Roman soldiers still appear in York?

It was later revealed that in 1957 another person had also witnessed the ghosts. Joan Mawson, a housekeeper in the house, saw a number of Roman soldiers either on horseback or on foot in the cellar and corridors. On the first occasion, she was alerted to their presence by the barking and snarling of her two Yorkshire Terriers who had run on before her down one of the corridors. Her descriptions tallied with Harry's in every detail, even down to the weary and unkempt look of the figures. She also described them as being splattered with mud and noted that the soldiers were slumped over their horses' necks. None appeared to be aware of her. In all, she saw them on three separate occasions over a 12-month period. She only revealed her story after Harry went public with his. It also emerged that Joan's daughter had heard the sound of the trumpet on more than one occasion.

It is also said the soldiers were seen in the 1930s and 40s – once by a visiting academic – but I have been unable to track down any first-hand accounts of this.

Since 1957 no one has reported seeing Roman figures in the house. So will they appear again? The cellar where Harry and Joan saw the soldiers was later altered, the original barrel roof being replaced by a new ceiling. I have often found that alterations to buildings can sometimes erase a haunting for good. It could be that Harry Martindale and Joan Mawson were destined to be the last two people ever to see the ghosts of York's first inhabitants and thus experience this unique snapshot from our Roman past.

Chapter 5

THE GREY MAN OF BEN MACDHUI

The forbidding mountain known as Ben MacDhui can be found in the Cairngorms in Scotland. For decades it has been known as the haunt of a spirit or creature known as the Big Grey Man or the Fear Liath Mor.

In 1891 Norman Collier, regarded as one of the greatest climbers of his generation and later a professor of organic chemistry at the University of London and a Fellow of the Royal Society, was climbing alone on the mountain. He later recalled what happened at the 27th Annual General Meeting of the Cairngorm Club in Aberdeen in December 1925:

> I was returning from the cairn on the summit in a mist when I began to think I heard something else than merely the noise of my own footsteps. For every few steps I took I heard a crunch and then another crunch as if someone was walking after me but taking steps three or four times the length of my own. I said to myself 'This is all nonsense'. I listened and heard it again but could see nothing in the mist. As I walked on and the eerie crunch, crunch sounded behind me I was seized with terror and took to my heels, staggering blindly among the boulders for four or five miles nearly down to Rothiemurchus Forest. Whatever you make of it I do not know, but there is something very queer about the top of Ben MacDhui and I will not go back there again by myself I know.

The press soon seized upon his story, which resulted in a flood of correspondence in the papers, with some suggesting that the professor's experience was due to nerves or even the sound of his footsteps echoing upon nearby rocks. Others countered this by stating that he was a man used to climbing alone and so could not be described as the sort to imagine or misinterpret such things.

The professor's experience on the mountain led to W.G. Robertson sending a letter to the Aberdeen Press and Journal in December 1925. This concerned the mountaineer Dr Kellas, who had died in 1921 during an expedition on Mount Everest:

The correspondence in your paper on the subject of the Ferla Mohr has encouraged me to state the story given to me by the late Mr Henry Kellas, my lifelong friend, with whom I once climbed Ben MacDhui. He and his brother, Dr Kellas, had been chipping for crystals in the late afternoon well below the cairn, and were together on the slope of a fold of the hill. Suddenly they became aware of a giant figure coming down towards them from the cairn. They saw it pass out of sight in the dip on the side of the fold remote from themselves, and awaited its reappearance. But fear possessed them ere it did reach the top, and they fled. They were aware it was following them, and tore down by Corrie Erchachan to escape it.

Mr Kellas said there was mist on part of the hill, but refused to believe that the figure could be the shadow of either his brother or himself, causing an optical illusion. He asked why not two figures if that had been the case. But he never spoke of 'crunching' or of footsteps being heard by either himself or his brother.

No one who knew Mr Kellas or heard him relate his story could doubt his complete faith in his experience.

The legend of the Grey Man soon became part of the folklore of the Cairngorms and over the years various other people reported seeing and hearing strange things on the mountain.

In the 1939 book *Always a Little Further*, Alastair Borthwick mentions the Grey Man and recounts the experiences of two friends:

The first was alone, heading over MacDhui for Corrour on a night when the snow had a hard, crisp crust through which his boots broke at every step. He reached the summit and it was while he was descending the slopes which fall towards the Larig that he heard footsteps behind him, *footsteps not in the rhythm of his own, but occurring only once for every three steps he took.*

'I felt a queer crinkly feeling in the back of my neck,' he told me, but I said to myself, 'this is silly, there must be a reason for it.' So I stopped, and the footsteps stopped, and I sat down and tried to reason it out. I could see nothing. There was a moon about somewhere, but the mist was fairly thick. The only thing I could make of it was that when my boots broke through the snow-crust they made some sort of echo. But then every step should have echoed, and not just this regular one-in-three. I was scared stiff. I got up, and walked on, trying hard not to look behind me. I got down all right – the footsteps stopped a thousand feet above the Larig – and I didn't run. But if anything had so much as said 'Boo!' behind me, I'd have been down to Corrour like a streak of lightning!

The second man's experience was roughly similar. He was on MacDhui, and alone. He heard footsteps. He was climbing in daylight, in summer; but so dense was the mist that he was working by compass, and visibility was almost as poor as it would have been at night. The footsteps he heard were made by something or someone trudging up the fine screes which decorate the upper parts of the mountain, a thing not extraordinary in itself, though the steps were only a few yards behind him, but exceedingly odd when the mist suddenly cleared and he could see no living thing on the mountain, at that point devoid of cover of any kind.

'Did the steps follow yours exactly?' I asked him. 'No,' he said. 'That was the funny thing. They didn't. They were regular all right; but the queer thing was that they seemed to come once for every two and a half steps I took.' He thought it queerer still when I told him the other man's story. You see, he was long-legged and six feet tall, and the first man was only five-feet-seven.

Once I was out with a search party on MacDhui; and on the way down after an unsuccessful day I asked some of the gamekeepers and stalkers who were with us what they thought of it all. They worked on

MacDhui, so they should know. Had they seen Ferlas Mor? Did he exist, or was it just a silly story? They looked at me for a few seconds, and then one said, 'We do not talk about that.'

In October 1943, the naturalist and climber Alexander Tewnion found himself alone on the mountain. He had taken a revolver with him in the hope of shooting some game in order to enrich his meagre wartime rations. He climbed to the summit of Ben MacDhui but noticed a storm was brewing and so began to descend the mountain using one of the tracks. He suddenly noticed the sound of footfalls behind him and what struck him was the long intervals between each footfall. He later recalled what happened in the *Scots Magazine* in June 1958:

I am not unduly imaginative, but my thought flashed instantly to the well-known story of Professor Collier and the Fear Liath Mor. Then I felt the reassuring weight of the loaded revolver in my pocket. Grasping the butt, I peered about in the mist here rent and tattered by the eddies of wind. A strange shape loomed up, receded, came charging at me! Without hesitation I whipped out the revolver and fired three times at the figure. When it still came on I turned and hared down the path, reaching Glen Derry in a time that I have never bettered.

You may ask was it really the Fear Laith Mor? Frankly, I think it was. Many times since then I have traversed MacDhui in the mist, bivouacked out in the open, camped on its summit for days on end on different occasions – often alone, and always with an easy mind. For on that day I am convinced I shot the only Fear Liath Mor my imagination will ever see.

In May 1945 another mountaineer by the name of Peter Densham also found himself on the summit of Ben MacDhui. He had heard talk of the Grey Man but had dismissed such things as the stuff of legend and gossip. He was busily eating some chocolate when …

I had the sudden impression there was someone near me – an impression which is sometimes experienced by mountaineers. I did not pay much attention to the impression knowing it was fairly common. After a little I had the impression of something cold on top of my neck. I had the hood of my anorak down. I thought this feeling of cold was due to the air having become more moist, but I still seemed to feel a pressure on my neck. I stood up and was conscious of a crunching noise from the direction of the cairn on my left. I went forward to investigate this noise. When I got nearer to this cairn I began to think of the Grey Man and his footsteps. I thought this experience very interesting and until within a few feet of the apparent source of the sound I was not the least frightened. Suddenly, however, I was overcome by a feeling of apprehension and after a little my overpowering wish was to get off the mountain. I found myself running at an incredible pace, and then realised that I was running in the direction of Lurcher's Crag. I tried to stop myself and found that it was extremely difficult to do. It was as if someone was pushing me. I managed to deflect my course, but with a great deal of difficulty.

Another time, Densham was on the mountain with his friend Richard Frere. They were both looking for a plane which had allegedly crashed in the area. They arrived at the summit at 4pm and sat for a while gazing at the view. Densham then realised that Frere was talking to someone:

I went round [to where Frere was] and found myself joining in the conversation. It was a strange experience which seemed to have a psychic aspect. We talked to someone invisible for some time, and it seemed we had carried on this conversation for some little time when we suddenly realised that there was no one there but ourselves. Afterwards, neither of us, strangely, could recall the purport of this extraordinary conversation!

Densham often returned to the mountain but never again experienced any strange phenomena. He was always convinced that his experiences were psychic in nature and went on record as stating that Ben MacDhui was 'the most mysterious mountain I have ever been on.'

Richard Frere also experienced something in 1948 when climbing the Cairngorms on his own. He was suddenly filled with depression and apathy and then became aware of being accompanied by an unseen presence. He also heard a high singing note which seemed to be coming from the very heart of the mountains. The sound and presence remained with him for hours, even to the very summit of Ben MacDhui. On his descent it remained with him, although the music become fainter with every step. The presence lingered on for some time and Frere had the feeling that it was desperate and was clinging to him in the hope it could finally escape the desolate mountain forever. He also felt that it could not do so as it was bound to the area by 'something terribly strong and utterly final'. Suddenly a flash of terror filled Frere's mind and the presence was gone.

Frere also revealed that a friend had agreed to spend a night alone on the mountain on the strength of a wager that he would not last the night before fleeing. The man, who Frere declined to name, made his way to the summit one cold, clear January evening. After putting up his tent and drinking some tea, he retired to his sleeping bag. He soon began to be filled with fear and strange thoughts of being the unwilling recipient of thoughts from a mind neither human, nor anti-human. He then fell asleep but was later woken by an ever-greater fear than before. The moonlight was shining through a crack in the tent when he suddenly noticed that one edge of the moonbeam had blurred due to something standing between the tent and the moon. He suddenly felt like a hunted animal and he stopped breathing in the hope that whatever it was would not hear him. The thing then vanished and the moonbeam shone white as before.

After recovering from shock, he opened the flysheet of the tent and looked out. About 20 feet away he saw a large brown creature 'swaggering' down the mountain. He described how the creature rolled slightly from side to side. It was covered in brown hair, had a large head with a thick neck and from the slimness of the hips appeared to be male. The creature walked upright and appeared to be at least 24 to 30 feet tall! The creature continued towards a gully and then vanished. Frere's friend bravely searched the gully but could find no trace of the creature.

Wendy Wood, in her book *The Secret of Spey*, also admits to an uncanny encounter on the pass of Lairig Ghru which lies below the mountain. She had been walking when she suddenly heard a voice of 'gigantic resonance' speaking behind her. It seemed to speak in Gaelic but she was too scared to listen to the exact words. She tried to convince herself that it was just a deer's bark but soon changed her mind when the voice started to come from beneath her very feet. She tried to explain this by searching the ground in circles to see if someone was lying trapped beneath the snow. The search proved fruitless and she suddenly became filled with fear and the desire to leave the area. She became aware of footsteps following her until she reached lower ground.

Joan Grant, the author of several books on reincarnation, had a particularly unnerving experience while walking below the mountain near Aviemore:

I was seized with such terror that I turned and in panic fled back along the path. Leslie (her husband) ran after me, imploring me to tell him what was wrong, I could only spare breath enough to tell him to run faster, faster. Something – utterly malign, four-legged, and yet obscenely human, invisible and yet solid enough for me to hear the pounding of its hooves, was trying to reach me. If it did I should die, for I was far too frightened to know how to defend myself! I had run about half a mile when I burst through an invisible barrier behind which I knew I was safe. I knew I was safe now, although a second before I had been in mortal danger.

George Duncan, an Aberdeen advocate and Sheriff-Substitute of Aberdeen, had an equally frightening experience. This occurred around the year 1914. His account was published in a letter to The Scotsman in 1941. He and a friend, James A. Parker, were travelling down the Derry Road at dusk after climbing the hills:

All at once, I got the shock of my life by seeing before me a tall figure in a black robe – the conventional figure of the Devil himself, waving his arms, clad in long sleeves, moving towards me. I got such a shock that I felt what I have never felt before or since, a cold shiver running down my spine. In a minute or two the dog-cart turned a corner and the figure passed from view. Afterwards my friend asked me why I had so suddenly become silent (we were in the middle of a conversation), and I told him what I had seen.

I have often visited the spot since in the endeavour to locate trees, the waving branches of which might have explained the experience, but without any satisfactory result.

Other visitors to the mountain have reported hearing footsteps, music, talking and laughter when alone on the mountain. One visitor even claimed to have attempted a conversation with the entity.

In July 1948 Captain Sir Hugh Rankin and his wife, Lady Rankin, were cycling in the Highlands and found themselves passing along the Lairig Ghru pass. Both suddenly felt a presence.

My wife felt it as distinctly as I did. We turned round and there was the Presence. We were not the least afraid. Being Buddhists we at once knew who it was. We both knelt and made an obeisance.

He was between six feet three inches and six feet four inches. He was enormously broad – about 50 inches round the chest I should say. He had big limbs and big hands. He had also very big feet but they made no imprints, as it being July, there was no snow in the Lairig Ghru itself, although there was in the corries. His head was finely chiselled. His nose was neither aquiline nor Roman but was cast in the Indo-Aryan mould. He was olive in complexion. He had long flowing locks of medium dark hair. He was dressed in a long robe like people wear in the East, and had on sandals.

It should be stressed at this point that the couple were convinced the entity was a Bodhisattva, a person who has achieved Enlightenment or Buddhahood, but has vowed to return to this world to aid all human beings on their paths to Buddhahood.

Sir Hugh later said that the being appeared to speak in Sanskit: 'I could not understand what he was saying, but I replied in Urdu, the only Eastern language I know. I said: "I bow to the Lord Bodhisattva who rules the destinies of the world."'

Sir Hugh said the entity stayed with them for some ten minutes before vanishing. Lady Rankin confirmed this and also said that rays of light had seemed to exude from the figure as he spoke. Music from bagpipes and Indian and other Eastern instruments could also be heard coming from the sky.

Strange things still continued to be heard and seen on Ben MacDhui. In December 2005 a film crew were making a short film about the Grey Man. One of the team, Peter George, was standing alone outside a stone shelter hut in the Lairig Ghru, when, 'out of the corner of my eye, over to the left towards the stream, I caught a glimpse of a tall grey figure. At first I thought it was one of our party, although all of them were inside the bothy. I turned to look properly and couldn't see anyone.'

So what are we to make of the Grey Man of Ben MacDhui? It is simply a case that defies any attempt at classification. The sightings range from a Yeti-like creature to a Buddhist Bodhisattva. Sceptics claim that the Grey Man is nothing more than an hallucination brought on by exhaustion, oxygen starvation, suggestion or even shadows on the mist (a phenomena known as the Brocken Spectre where the sun projects the shadow of a climber onto nearby mists or clouds). They also state that the sounds of footsteps, laughter and music can be explained away by the sounds of animals and the wind distorted by the acoustic properties of the rocks and gullies.

Those who believe in the Grey Man point out that no other mountain in Scotland has a reputation for being haunted. So why are climbers not experiencing similar things on other mountains if it is all just a case of exhaustion or hallucination brought on by lack of oxygen? For instance, Ben Nevis is higher and yet has no reputation of being haunted. They also point to the fact that many of those who witnessed strange phenomena on Ben MacDhui were experienced climbers and were hardly the sort to imagine things to the point of being scared by their own shadow or the echo of their footsteps.

I personally feel that there is something strange on that mountain. Are we dealing with a being or elemental that can somehow appear to different people in different ways? Maybe Richard Frere was not so far from the truth when he felt that the 'presence' was bound to the mountain in some terrible way and could never leave. If so, it deserves our pity rather than our fear.

Chapter 6

THE CURSE OF WILLIAM CORDER'S SKULL

T he Red Barn Murder was a crime which shocked the whole nation in 1828. It was in the Suffolk village of Polstead that Maria Marten met her gruesome end at the hands of her lover, William Corder. The case had all the ingredients needed to satisfy the public – a fallen woman, a wicked farmer's son and a grieving mother who had the murder revealed to her in a dream. Indeed, the case became so notorious in the 19th century that it inspired plays, books and china figures of the murderer, his victim and even the very place of her death!

Maria and William both lived in Polstead and had been having an affair for some time. Maria had become pregnant by her lover but the child had died

William Corder's house in Polstead. (Julie Abbott)

Maria Marten's cottage in Polstead. (Julie Abbott)

when it was just two months old. It was later rumoured that the child had been killed by poison and secretly buried by the couple in a nearby field.

Corder soon tired of Maria and her constant pleadings to become his wife. He finally decided to end the relationship and enticed her to the

MARIA MARTEN.

WILLIAM CORDER.

Red Barn (a farm building owned by his family) on 18 May 1827 with the promise that he would take her to Ipswich to get married. The exact circumstances of her death are not clear, but it does appear that Corder both stabbed and shot Maria. He then buried her in the barn, concealing the grave with hay.

Corder left the area and eventually found himself living in London. He wrote letters to Maria's family claiming that Maria was now his wife but made various excuses as to why they had not heard from her – she had been ill, she had been unable to write due to an injured hand or her letters had got lost in the post.

Maria's stepmother, Ann Marten, became deeply troubled by Corder's excuses and in March 1828 claimed she had dreamt on three successive nights that her stepdaughter was buried in the Red Barn. At her insistence, her husband went to the barn and dug at the spot indicated in his wife's dreams. He soon came upon Maria's rotting body. She was identified by her hair, clothing and a missing tooth. Corder's handkerchief was discovered tied around the body's neck

A correct View of the Exterior.

THE RED BARN AT POLSTEAD

A search was made for Corder and he was finally tracked down to a boarding house in Ealing. Corder was running a school for young ladies with his new wife, Mary Moore, whom he had met through a newspaper advertisement in The Times newspaper.

Corder was taken back to Suffolk to face trial in Bury St Edmunds. During the trial, Corder claimed that Maria had committed suicide and in a panic he had hidden the body for fear of being accused of her murder. Needless to say, the jury was not impressed and Corder was sentenced to hang. Corder, realising that the game was up, then made a full confession in which he admitted killing his lover. His execution attracted over 7,000 people and afterwards it is recorded that thousands of men and women queued up to view Corder's body after it was cut down from the scaffold. He was then given over to the medical profession for dissection.

CONFESSION AND EXECUTION OF
WILLIAM CORDER,
THE MURDERER OF MARIA MARTEN.

Since the tragical affair between Thurtell and Weare, no event has occurred connected with the criminal annals of our country which has excited so much interest as the trial of Corder, who was justly convicted of the murder of Maria Marten on Friday last.

THE CONFESSION.

"Bury Gaol, August 10th, 1828.—Condemned cell.
"Sunday evening, half-past Eleven.

"I acknowledge being guilty of the death of poor Maria Marten, by shooting her with a pistol. The particulars are as follows:—When we left her father's house, we began quarrelling about the burial of the child: she apprehended the place wherein it was deposited would be found out. The quarrel continued about three quarters of an hour upon this sad and about other subjects. A scuffle ensued, and during the scuffle, and at the time I think that she had hold of me, I took the pistol from the side pocket of my velveteen jacket and fired. She fell, and died in an instant. I never saw her even struggle. I was overwhelmed with agitation and dismay:—the body fell near the front doors on the floor of the barn. A vast quantity of blood issued from the wound, and ran on to the floor and through the crevices. Having determined to bury the body in the barn (about two hours after she was dead, I went and borrowed a spade of Mrs Stow, but before I went there I dragged the body from the barn into the chaff-house, and locked the barn. I returned again to the barn, and began to dig a hole, but the spade being a bad one, and the earth firm and hard, I was obliged to go home for a pickaxe and a better spade, with which I dug the hole, and then buried the body. I think I dragged the body by the handkerchief that was tied round her neck. It was dark when I finished covering up the body. I went the next day, and washed the blood from off the barn-floor. I declare to Almighty God I had no sharp instrument about me, and no other wound but the one made by the pistol was inflicted by me. I have been guilty of great idleness, and at times led a dissolute life, but I hope through the mercy of God to be forgiven. WILLIAM CORDER."

Witness to the signing by the said William Corder,
JOHN ORRIDGE.

Condemned cell, Eleven o'clock, Monday morning, August 11th, 1828.

The above confession was read over carefully to the prisoner in our presence, who stated most solemnly it was true, and that he had nothing to add to or retract from it.—W. STOCKING, chaplain ; TIMOTHY R. HOLMES, Under-Sheriff.

THE EXECUTION.

At ten minutes before twelve o'clock the prisoner was brought from his cell and pinioned by the hangman, who was brought from London for the purpose. He appeared resigned, but was so weak as to be unable to stand without support; when his cravat was removed he groaned heavily, and appeared to be labouring under great mental agony. When his wrists and arms were made fast, he was led round towards the scaffold, and as he passed the different yards in which the prisoners were confined, he shook hands with them, and speaking to two of them by name, he said, "Good bye, God bless you." They appeared considerably affected by the wretched appearance which he made, and "God bless you!" "May God receive your soul!" were frequently uttered as he passed along. The chaplain walked before the prisoner, reading the usual Burial Service, and the Governor and Officers walking immediately after him. The prisoner was supported to the steps which led to the scaffold; he looked somewhat wildly around, and a constable was obliged to support him while the hangman was adjusting the fatal cord. There was a barrier to keep off the crowd, amounting to upwards of 7,000 persons, who at this time had stationed themselves in the adjoining fields, on the hedges, the tops of houses, and at every point from which a view of the execution could be best obtained. The prisoner, a few moments before the drop fell, groaned heavily, and would have fallen, had not a second constable caught hold of him. Everything having been made ready, the signal was given, the fatal drop fell, and the unfortunate man was launched into eternity. Just before he was turned off, he said in a feeble tone, "I am justly sentenced, and may God forgive me."

The Murder of Maria Marten.
BY W. CORDER.

COME all you thoughtless young men, a warning take by me,
And think upon my unhappy fate to be hanged upon a tree;
My name is William Corder, to you I do declare,
I courted Maria Marten, most beautiful and fair.

I promised I would marry her upon a certain day,
Instead of that, I was resolved to take her life away.
I went into her father's house the 18th day of May,
Saying, my dear Maria, we will fix the wedding day.

If you will meet me at the Red-barn, as sure as I have life,
I will take you to Ipswich town, and there make you my wife;
I then went home and fetched my gun, my pickaxe and my spade,
I went into the Red-barn, and there I dug her grave.

With heart so light, she thought no harm, to meet him she did go
He murdered her all in the barn, and laid her body low;
After the horrible deed was done, she lay weltering in her gore,
Her bleeding mangled body he buried beneath the Red-barn floor.

Now all things being silent, her spirit could not rest,
She appeared unto her mother, who suckled her at her breast ;
For many a long month or more, her mind being sore oppress'd,
Neither night or day she could not take any rest.

Her mother's mind being so disturbed, she dreamt three nights o'er,
Her daughter she lay murdered beneath the Red-barn floor;
She sent the father to the barn, when he the ground did thrust,
And there he found his daughter mingling with the dust.

My trial is hard, I could not stand, most woeful was the sight,
When her jaw-bone was brought to prove, which pierced my heart quite ;
Her aged father standing by, likewise his loving wife,
And in her grief her hair she tore, she scarcely could keep life.

Adieu, adieu, my loving friends, my glass is almost run,
On Monday next will be my last, when I am to be hang'd ;
So you, young men, who do pass by, with pity look on me,
For murdering Maria Marten, I was hang'd upon the tree.

Printed by J. Catnach, 2 and 3, Monmouth Court.—Cards, &c., Printed Cheap.

189

The confession and execution of William Corder as recorded in a broadsheet of the time. (public domain)

67

Gruesome electrical experiments were carried out on the corpse using a galvanic battery. A death mask was also taken of him. These were often used in phrenology – the study of the shape and size of the cranium as a supposed indication of character and mental abilities. Corder was asserted to be profoundly developed in the areas of 'secretiveness, acquisitiveness, destructiveness, philoprogenitiveness, and imitativeness with little evidence of benevolence or veneration.' Corder's skeleton was later given to the West Suffolk Hospital where it was used in anatomy lessons. Part of Corder's skin was even used to bind a book about the trial.

The fact that Maria's stepmother had dreamed her stepdaughter had been buried in the Red Barn has always fascinated students of the paranormal. So did Maria's spirit really reveal her murder by making her stepmother dream of her burial or did Ann Marten lie about the dreams in order to find an excuse for the barn floor to be dug up? Some historians have speculated that the stepmother was also having an affair with Corder – she was only a year older than Maria. Was she a willing accomplice in her stepdaughter's murder in order to remove her rival for Corder's affections? It is also alleged that Ann Marten only decided to claim supernatural assistance after she discovered that Corder had married and was obviously not coming back to her. It should be recorded that the Marten household possessed a book entitled *The Old English Baron* in which the location of a woman's body is revealed by her mother's dream. Coincidence?

It has to be said that Corder never once sort to implicate the stepmother, nor was it ever suggested in court that Ann Marten was involved in the crime. It should be noted that she was apparently deeply troubled by Maria's failure to write to the family. She had also heard Corder arrange to meet Maria in the Red Barn on the very day that she had last been seen. Did these factors play upon her mind and cause her to dream of murder and concealment? But even that theory still does not explain how Ann knew exactly where to dig for the body. Her direct involvement in the crime or a psychic intervention via a dream cannot be ruled out.

Maria Marten's memorial in St Mary's churchyard. (John West)

Corder's skeleton continued to reside in the West Suffolk Hospital Museum where it remained an object of morbid curiosity for staff and visitors alike. Corder's scalp and the book bound in his skin took a different route and in the 1870s found themselves in the possession of a certain Dr

John Kilner. He had a fascination for the case and decided to enhance his murder collection by acquiring Corder's skull. That it was held by the hospital did not trouble the good doctor as he reasoned that one skull is very much like another – he would simply replace Corder's skull with a similar one! Kilner soon set his plan in motion and late one evening sneaked into the dark and deserted museum to claim his prize. It was not long before he found himself in front of Corder's skeleton, lighting three candles to illuminate the morbid object of his desires. As soon as all three were lit, the first candle was mysteriously snuffed out. As he relit it, the other two were also extinguished. Kilner, unnerved by this, quickly set to work removing the skull and replacing it with a duplicate. The candles continued to act strangely, only one managing to stay lit, and the doctor was deeply relieved when he was finally able to leave the museum with his prize.

Dr Kilner returned home and had the skull polished, mounted and placed in an ebony box in his drawing room. However, the incident of the candles still troubled him and he later admitted to a friend that he could not shake off a feeling of unease since taking the skull.

One evening, a few days later, after surgery, Kilner's maid came in and said that a gentleman wished to see him. The doctor was somewhat irritated by this late caller and asked the maid if she had seen the man before. 'No,' replied the maid, adding that the man was 'proper old-fashioned looking, wearing a furry top hat and a blue overcoat with silver buttons.'

The doctor asked the maid to fetch a lamp and went to the surgery to meet the stranger. Upon entering the room, he thought he saw a figure standing by the window. The maid then entered with the lamp. Both were surprised to find the now illuminated room empty. The doctor was far from happy and accused the maid of dreaming the whole thing up. She stuck to her story and suggested that the man had simply changed his mind about seeing the doctor and left.

The incident was soon forgotten and things returned to normal in the house. Then, one evening on looking out from his drawing room window,

Kilner thought he spotted a man hiding by the summerhouse at the end of the lawn. The figure appeared to be wearing an old fashioned hat and a greatcoat. The doctor rushed out to find out what the man was doing but found he had disappeared.

The doctor was then reminded of the strange behaviour of the candles in the museum and the disappearance of the mysterious stranger in his surgery a few nights before. Could these be linked to the skull? Kilner became convinced that someone or something was dogging his steps and desired to communicate with him urgently. He also felt that whatever it was lacked the power to do so.

Tensions now began to grow as a presence made itself known in the house. Doors were suddenly opened and footsteps heard. Members of the household heard loud hammering and sobbing in the room where the skull was kept. They also claimed to have heard heavy breathing and muttering noises outside their rooms. The doctor also started to have bad dreams in which he felt that a presence was pleading with him to listen and attend his needs.

Kilner was now convinced that the skull was somehow responsible for the disturbances and resolved to get rid of it. He thought of returning it to the museum but realised that the now highly polished and darkened skull would immediately be noticed if he attempted to reunite it with the rest of Corder's skeleton.

The next night, the doctor decided to leave his bedroom door open so that he would be immediately aware of any presence or sudden noise in the house. He soon feel asleep but was disturbed a few hours later by sounds from downstairs. He got up, lit a candle, and made his way to the landing. He looked over the stair-rail and noticed that a white hand was holding the handle door of the drawing room. To his horror, he saw that the hand possessed no body!

The door handle turned and suddenly the whole house was shaken by the sound of a blunderbuss being fired. Grabbing another candlestick as a weapon, Kilner rushed downstairs and entered the drawing room. He was met by a rush of wind which seemed to envelope him like a shroud. He lit a match and saw on the floor a scatter of wood fragments. The box in which the skull had been stored had been smashed to pieces. His eyes then travelled to the cabinet. The door was open, and there, on the shelf, was the skull.

This was the final straw. Kilner offered the skull to his friend, Frederick Hopkins. Hopkins had been an official with the Commission of Prisons and had bought part of the old Bury Jail, Gyves House, when the prison had closed in 1877.

Kilner apparently failed to warn Hopkins of the incidents connected with the skull – some friend! Upon handing over the skull he said, 'As you are the owner of Corder's condemned cell and the gallows on which he was hanged, perhaps it won't hurt you to take care of the skull!'

Hopkins gladly accepted the gift and wrapped it in a silk handkerchief. Later that same evening, Hopkins was walking down the steps of the Angel Hotel in Bury when he tripped and twisted his foot. The skull rolled out from beneath the handkerchief and ended up at the feet of a lady walking by. You can imagine her response upon seeing the grinning skull looking up at her! It took Hopkins a week to recover from the fall. How long it took the lady to recover is sadly not recorded.

Over the following weeks one disaster followed another – Hopkins's favourite horse fell to its death in a chalk pit, property and land deals arranged with Dr Kilner went sour and both came to the brink of financial ruin.

Hopkins also became convinced that the skull was the cause of all his recent troubles and became determined to dispose of it. He took it to a churchyard near Bury St Edmunds and bribed a gravedigger to bury it in consecrated ground. After this, all his troubles ceased. Dr Kilner's fortunes also took a turn for the better. One can only hope that his experiences with Corder's skull finally persuaded the good doctor that acquiring medical exhibits without permission was one hobby best forgotten.

William Corder. (pubic domain)

The tale of Corder's skull was later told to Hopkins's son, Thurston, who made himself quite a name as an author and ghost hunter and it is through him that the curse of Corder's skull became known to a wider audience.

So what of the rest of Corder's skeleton, his scalp and the book bound in his skin? The skeleton remained at the West Suffolk Hospital where it is recorded that trainee doctors and nurses would often take Corder's mortal remains to hospital dances for a spin on the dance floor. In 1947 the skeleton was moved to the Royal Hunterian Museum in London. In 2004 it was handed over to one of Corder's descendants and consigned to a crematorium after a brief service. Corder's scalp and the book now reside in Moyses Hall Museum in Bury St Edmunds, along with other Corder relics including his death mask and the pistols used to dispatch Maria to the next world. Although the museum is supposedly haunted, no supernatural activity has been recorded in the vicinity of the Corder exhibits.

So is Corder's spirit finally at rest? I can but offer you the following warning from Mr Thurston Hopkins ... 'if you ever come across a tortoiseshell tinted skull in a japanned cash box leave it severely alone. If you take it home there will be the Devil to Pay – and you may not be prepared to meet his bill.'

Chapter 7

GHOSTS OF THE BLOODY TOWER

The Tower of London has been a place of imprisonment, torture and execution for centuries. It is even said that the very mortar used to build the White Tower was mixed with blood from William the Conqueror's Saxon victims. Its reputation as the most haunted castle in Britain is certainly well deserved and any would-be ghost hunter going there can expect to encounter executed royalty, phantom bears, shapeless forms and even the screaming victims of torture within its ancient walls.

Every part of the Tower complex can boast at least one ghost or odd happening. Here are some of the most fascinating.

A Colonel E. H. Carkeet James once wrote of a soldier of the 60th Rifles who had faced court-martial in 1864 after he was found unconscious during his watch outside the Queen's House. The soldier claimed that he had seen a white figure moving towards him. He had called out a challenge and then charged at the apparition with his bayonet drawn, fainting as his weapon passed through the figure. Two other soldiers corroborated his story – they had both witnessed the incident from a window in the Bloody Tower – and the sentry was acquitted. The figure has been seen by other guards, including one who saw a white form, accompanied by the sound of clicking heels on the stone floor. Upon reaching a patch of moonlight, he saw that the figure was headless. It is thought by some that this may be the ghost of Anne Boleyn – the ill-fated

The sounds of Guy Fawkes being tortured have been heard in the Queen's House. (public domain)

75

An execution at the Tower. (public domain)

wife of Henry VIII – who spent her last night on earth in the Queen's House.

The house is also said to be haunted by the sounds of chanting, footsteps and the groans of someone being tortured – Guy Fawkes was 'examined' there. A room which adjoins the one where Anne was held is noticeably

Anne Boleyn's ghost has been seen haunting the Tower grounds. (public domain)

colder than the rest of the building. The smell of perfume has also been noticed on more than one occasion and people sleeping in the room have experienced a sensation of being slowly suffocated.

In 1972 a nine-year-old girl called Joan actually claimed to have witnessed the final moments of Anne Boleyn. She was on holiday with her parents and was visiting the Tower for the very first time. A guide was talking about the various people executed with an axe on Tower Green, including Anne Boleyn, when the girl whispered to her mother, 'They didn't chop off her head with an axe. They did it with a sword.' She later gave more details, including the fact that the executioner had removed his shoes and crept up behind the queen to behead her. Her father maintained that his daughter had no interest in history and had never read any books or seen any programmes devoted to the Tudors.

In 1975 several personnel in the Waterloo Barracks were woken up by terrible screams that appeared to come from Tower Green. The sounds were also heard by soldiers in the nearby Byward Tower. More screams were heard a few days later by a soldier patrolling the area. Searches failed to provide an explanation. It has been suggested that the screams may have been the harrowing death agonies of Margaret Pole, Countess of Salisbury. The Countess was over 70 years of age and had been condemned to death by Henry VIII after her son – safe on the continent – had attacked the King's religious policies. The Countess refused to submit meekly to the axe and the executioner was forced to chase her round the block, literally hacking her to death as, screaming, she tried to evade the blows.

The Tower Chapel of St Peter ad Vincula contains the bodies of many of the victims executed in the Tower, including Anne Boleyn. Henry's contempt for his former love did not end with her death and her headless corpse was unceremoniously thrown into an old arrow chest and buried in the crypt.

One evening in the 19th century an officer was making his rounds with a sentry when he saw a light in the chapel. He asked the sentry about it and the soldier replied that he had often seen a light there. The officer found a ladder and used it to climb up and look into the building. He never forgot what he saw.

Walking slowly down the central aisle were a number of ladies and knights. They were led by a female whose features and dress resembled portraits of Anne Boleyn. The figures repeatedly paced the chapel and then, along with the light, suddenly vanished.

At least one soldier has died as a result of his experiences in the Tower. In January 1815 a sentry suddenly saw the shadowy shape of a bear near the door of the Martin Tower. He lunged at it with his bayonet but the weapon harmlessly passed through the creature and smashed into the door.

The Tower of London. (John West)

The sentry died of shock two days later but only after telling his comrades of his encounter. The Tower once housed a royal menagerie, including bears. One was even led out on a chain and allowed to catch fish in the

Thames. So did the soldier witness the phantom of a former royal pet?

The Martin Tower was also the scene of the most baffling haunting – if indeed it was a haunting – in the whole history of the Tower.

It was October 1817 and Edward Lenthal Swifte, the Keeper of the Crown Jewels, was having supper with his family when he witnessed something that still defies explanation to this day. He later wrote of his experience in an 1860 publication called Notes & Queries:

> In 1814 I was appointed Keeper of the Crown Jewels in the Tower, where I resided with my family till my retirement in 1852. One Saturday night in October, 1817, about the 'witching hour', I was at supper with my wife, her sisters, and our little boy, in the sitting room of the Jewel House, which – then comparatively modernised – is said to have been the 'doleful prison' of Anne Boleyn and of the ten bishops whom Oliver Cromwell piously accommodated therein.
>
> The room was – as it still is – irregularly shaped, having three doors and two windows, which last are cut nearly nine feet deep into the outer wall; between these is a chimney piece, projecting far into the room, and (then) surmounted with a large oil-painting. On the night in question the doors were all closed, heavy and dark cloth curtains were let down over the windows, and the only light in the room was that of two candles on the table; I sat at the foot of the table, my son on the right hand, his mother fronting the chimney piece, and her sister on the opposite end. I had offered a glass of water and wine to my wife, when, on putting it to her lips, she paused, and exclaimed, 'Good God! what is that? I looked up and saw a cylindrical figure, like a glass tube, seemingly about the thickness of my arm, and hovering between the ceiling and the table; its contents appeared to be a dense fluid, white and pale azure, like the gathering of a summer cloud, and incessantly mingling within the cylinder. This lasted about two minutes, when it slowly began to move before my sister-in-law, then, following the oblong shape of the table, before my

son and myself; passing behind my wife, it paused for a moment over her right shoulder (observe, there was no mirror opposite to her in which she could there behold it). Instantly she crouched down, and with both hands covering her shoulder, she shrieked out, 'Oh, Christ! It has seized me! Even now, while writing, I feel the fresh horror of that moment. I caught up my chair, struck at the wainscot behind her, rushed upstairs to the other children's room, and told the terrified nurse what I had seen. Meanwhile the other domestics had hurried into the parlour, where the mistress recounted to them the scene, even as I was detailing it above stairs.

The marvel of all this is enhanced by the fact that neither my sister-in-law nor my son beheld this 'appearance'. When I, the next morning, related the night's horror to our chaplain, after the service in the Tower church, he asked me, might not one person have his natural senses deceived? And if one, why might not two? My answer was, if two, why not two thousand? An argument which would reduce history, secular or sacred, to a fable.

So what was it? Explanations range from a form of electrical disturbance such as ball lighting to a time-travelling probe from the future!

And finally …

Elliott O'Donnell, ghost hunter and author in the first decades of the 20th century, was told an amusing tale by one of the Tower Beefeaters:

Is the Tower of London haunted? … why of course it is! Haunted by all sorts of ghosts – legions of them! I remember one of them particularly well. It was when I was on duty in the Beauchamp Tower, just outside the cell where Anne Boleyn was imprisoned. I was thinking of old Henry VIII, and wishing I had his luck with wives, for my one and only old missus was as ugly as Newgate, when all of a sudden I heard my name called, and on turning round, nearly died with fright. Floating in mid-air, immediately behind me, was a face – God help me, it makes me shiver, even now, to think of it – round, red and bloated, with a loose,

Henry VIII is also said to haunt the Tower. (public domain)

dribbling mouth and protruding heavy-lidded, pale eyes, alight with a
lurid and perfectly 'ellish glow.

I knew the face at once, for I had often seen it in the history books
– 'Enery VIII. 'Enery with all the devil showing in him. I was so
scared that I ran, and did not stop running, till I came upon two of

my comrades, who were beginning to clamour out 'What's the matter?'
when they suddenly broke off – the face had followed me.

Well! to cut a long story short, the affair was hushed up and in the
usual way we were all threatened with the sack if we dare as much as
breathe a word that the Tower was 'aunted. The oddest thing about
it, 'owever, is, that on my return home, I found my missus was dead.
She had died at the very moment I saw the 'ead. I suppose old 'Arry
wanted her. Well, as far as I am concerned he's 'ighly welcomed to her.
At all events he'll never get rid of her. She'll stick to him like porous
plaster.

It looks like Henry VIII got his just desserts after all!

Chapter 8

THE HAIRY HANDS OF DARTMOOR

Dartmoor is a place steeped in legend and mystery. Phantom hounds, demons, witches, corpse lights and pixies are said to abound here. Sir Arthur Conan Doyle was even inspired to write The Hound of the Baskervilles after visiting the area and hearing of the various legends associated with the place. One can almost sense that the boundary between this world and the next has little meaning here and many visitors end up leaving the moors with a strange feeling of unease and foreboding.

One of Dartmoor's most puzzling and horrifying hauntings dates back to the last century and concerns a pair of huge hairy hands.

It was June 1921 and the Medical Officer of Dartmoor Prison, Dr E.H. Helby, found himself riding his motorbike along a lonely stretch of moorland road between Two Bridges and Postbridge, a road now known as the B3212 (also known as Carter's Road). He was accompanied in the sidecar by the two young daughters of the Deputy Prison Governor. They were travelling down a hill towards a small bridge which crossed the East Dart, a tributary of the River Dart, when he suddenly shouted to the children to jump clear. The terrified girls did so and were shocked to see the doctor apparently struggling with the handlebars before swerving off the road and crashing. He was tragically killed.

A few weeks later tragedy almost struck the area again when a coach driver lost control of his vehicle on the same stretch of road. Several of his passengers were thrown from their seats. The driver claimed that hairy hands had grabbed the wheel and forced the coach into a ditch.

Another incident occurred on 21 August when an unnamed army captain reported that he had fought to control his motorcycle after what appeared to be a pair of invisible hairy hands seized his own hands and forced him off the road. Here is his account as reported to the press of the time:

> *It was not my fault. Believe it or not, something drove me off the road. A pair of hairy hands closed over mine. I felt them as plainly as ever I felt anything in my life – large, muscular, hairy hands. I fought them for all I was worth, but they were too strong for me. They forced the machine into the turf at the edge of the road, and I knew no more till I came to myself, lying a few feet away on my face on the turf.*

Another motorcyclist also faced a similar experience when he found himself losing control of his vehicle at the very same spot. His passenger, riding pillion, reported that he had seen a hairy hand appear from nowhere. They grabbed the handlebars, forcing the bike off the road. The passenger was unhurt but the rider was killed.

It emerged that accidents involving cars, bikes and even horse-drawn carts and traps had been reported on the road as early as 1910. Witnesses claimed that something seemed to take hold of their hands and force them off the road. Horses would also rise up and panic as if they could sense something before them.

To make matters worse, it then emerged that the hands were not just confined to the road. In 1924 the folklorist Theo Brown, together with her mother and father, were camping on the moors near a ruined powder mill roughly half a mile from the road at a place known as Cherry Brook. Her mother had been sleeping when she suddenly awoke with a sense of foreboding:

> *I knew there was some power very seriously menacing us near, and I must act very swiftly. As I looked up to the little window at the end of the caravan, I saw something moving, and as I stared, I saw it was the fingers and palm of a very large hand with many hairs on the joints and back of it, clawing up and up to the top of the window, which was a little open. I knew it wished to do harm to my husband sleeping below. I knew that the owner of the hand hated us and wished harm,*

and I knew it was no ordinary hand, and that no blow or shot would have any power over it.

Almost unconsciously I made the Sign of the Cross and I prayed very much that we might be kept safe. At once the hand slowly sank down out of sight and I knew the danger was gone. I did say a thankful prayer and fell at once into a peaceful sleep. We stayed in that spot for several weeks but I never felt the evil influence again near the caravan. But, I did not feel happy in some places not far off and would not for anything have walked alone on the moor at night or on the Tor above our caravan.

Theo Brown also reported that a friend of hers, William Webb, was walking down the B3212 towards Postbridge when he heard a terrible scream coming from the moors. He claimed it was unlike any animal he had ever heard before. Needless to say, he hurried on, unwilling to investigate further.

It is interesting to note that Theo Brown's father and mother felt that the entity or 'influence' was gradually retreating northwards across the moor and that its power was strongest on the slope on the western side of Postbridge, roughly 100 yards above Drift Lane.

Following the first press reports of the apparent supernatural events occurring here, the road was examined and it was found that sections of the camber were unsafe and the road was altered. Sadly, any hope that the repairs would exercise the phantom would however prove forlorn as motorists still reported strange and frightening events along the road.

Michael Williams in his book *Supernatural Dartmoor* revealed that his friend, the journalist Rufus Engle, was driving towards Postbridge when 'suddenly, as I approached the bridge, a pair of hands gripped the driving wheel and I had to fight for control. It was a very scary minute or so. God knows how I didn't crash at the bridge, and the hands went as inexplicably as they came.' He requested that story not be published in his lifetime as he feared mockery from sceptics.

One lady, Florence Warwick, aged 28, had the misfortune to lose power in her car as she drove along the same stretch of road. She pulled out the car handbook and tried to ascertain what could be wrong. 'As I was reading in the failing light, a cold feeling suddenly came over me. I felt as if I was being watched. I looked up and saw a pair of huge, hairy hands pressed against the windscreen. I tried to scream, but couldn't. I was frozen with fear. It was horrible, they were just inches away. After what seemed a lifetime, I heard myself cry out and the hands seemed to vanish.' To her relief the car suddenly kicked back into life and she drove off.

In 1955 a cyclist, Maurice Dart, found himself cycling across Dartmoor one warm summer evening. He had passed through Postbridge and was heading towards Princetown down a tree-lined section of the road when he was suddenly seized by panic. Looking back he saw what seemed to be a swirling cloudy mass in the sky. To make matters worse, it was heading towards him! He quickly changed gear and peddled for his life through Two Bridges. The feeling of panic suddenly left him and looking back he saw that the cloudy mass was moving back up into the sky.

In the 1960s a car was found overturned by the road, the male owner dead in the wreckage. Examination of the car failed to provide a mechanical explanation for the crash. Another vehicle causing the accident was also ruled out. In 1977 a Somerset doctor was driving through Postbridge when he felt a strange and powerful force in his car. The interior became icy cold and he stopped the car. The feeling went and he drove off. Suddenly, the car was again filled with a malignant energy which the doctor described as being almost like a paralysis. 'I was aware of a great force or weight in the car, something quite out of my control.' He didn't see the hands but described how 'the steering wheel seemed to go wild and it was wrenched out of my hands.' He skidded across the road and finally found himself hanging from his seatbelt. He was shaken but unhurt.

Walkers have also reported a sudden sensation of unease and fear when using the road and in the 1990s a van driver returning home at night reported that shortly after spotting a figure by the road the vehicle started to swerve violently for no apparent reason. Looking down he saw to his horror a pair of hairy hands holding the wheel of the vehicle. He fought to regain control of the van but was unable to do so before it swerved off the road into the moor beyond. The hands then vanished. The man was unhurt but was understandably suffering from shock. He was unaware of the legend of the hands at the time of the accident. The last reported incident dates from January 2008 when a man named Michael found himself on the road one night. He suddenly felt cold and experienced a sense of evil in the car. He then found his hands and wheel grabbed by two large hairy hands which battled to force his car off the road. He managed to keep control of the wheel and the hands vanished in a blinding flash of light.

So what are we to make of the sinister events of the B3212? Sceptics claim that motorists were driving too fast and were bound to crash as they were unfamiliar with the bends and camber of the road. The story of the hands was therefore concocted in order to avoid accusations of dangerous driving. As the legend of the hairy hands became well-known any mishap was automatically blamed on the phantom. It is certainly possible that some of the accidents were due to bad driving but that would not explain the sighting by Theo Brown's mother in the caravan or those drivers who were unaware of the previous incidents and yet still reported a sensation of the wheel being grabbed by hands other than their own. It should also be noted that several of the reported accidents occurred on a supposedly safe straight stretch of the road between the Cherry Brook Bridge and Archerton turning.

For those who favour a supernatural explanation, it should be said that several local traditions point to a tragic event being responsible for the first appearance of the hands. One tale relates that in the early 19th century an escaped prisoner from Dartmoor Prison was killed on this road when he tried to seize the reins of a passing pony and trap. He slipped and was crushed under the wheels. Another story states that the hands belong to the spirit of an Edwardian who was killed when he lost control of his car near the bridge. He now supposedly seeks to send others to their death in frustration at being unable to leave this world. Others insist that it is an earthbound elemental or nature spirit, linked to one of the nearby ancient settlements or burial grounds, a being which resents the building of the road. Some have even suggested it is the spirit of a prehistoric ape man or even the phantom of a man blown to bits after sparks from his boots caused an explosion in the nearby powder mill. A search for his body resulted in the recovery of just his hands!

So is the road still haunted? Only time will tell. All I can say is that you will not catch me using the B3212 and I certainly have no plans to camp out on the windswept moors that border the road. But if you do happen to find yourself driving along this particular stretch of road, I will humbly offer you the following advice: slow down, keep your eyes fixed firmly on the road ahead, grip the steering wheel with both hands and, above all, remember the words of Sir Arthur Conan Doyle and 'avoid the moor in those hours of darkness when the powers of evil are exalted.'

Chapter 9

THE MONKS OF ST DUNSTAN'S

St Dunstan's in East Acton dates from 1879. A local tradition states that the land on which the Victorian building now stands once belonged to the medieval church of St Bartholomew the Great in London. It was further thought that an outpost of the church had been located in the area and a mansion later built nearby was named Friar's Place in honour of this long-standing belief.

The first account of a haunting connected with the church dates from one Sunday afternoon in the 1930s. The elderly curate, the Rev. Philip Boustead, was walking home with his assistant organist after a service. The organist casually discussed the history of the building but then noticed that his companion seemed preoccupied with something. The curate then spoke of his conviction that St Dunstan's was haunted:

> I must tell you something. I cannot tell anyone else, because they will laugh at me. There is something strange about our church. I have seen things when I've been alone in there. Some of these old monks who used to live round here. No, no – I don't want to say any more, but I know there is something there. Now please don't tell anyone else what I have been saying. They'll think I'm mad.

The surprised organist agreed to keep the matter private and only revealed their conversation after the haunting became well-known in the following years.

It was the winter of 1937/38 and the nearby vicarage of St Gabriel's also became the setting for alleged spirit activity. The building was up for sale and the vicar, the Rev. G. V. Camplin-Cogan – a sceptic when it came to the paranormal – admitted that several visitors had heard strange noises,

St Dunstan's. (public domain)

including footsteps on the stairs. His wife had also heard the footsteps but upon investigating the source had found the stairs and hall empty. One visitor had even seen a monk-like figure in one of the bedrooms. It was said that centuries ago a monk had been buried under a cobbled path near the vicarage and it was surmised by some that his spirit was responsible for the disturbances.

Six years were to pass before any further ghosts were reported in the area. It was December 1944 and the Rev. Hugh Harold Anton-Stephens became the new vicar of St Dunstan's. He was in his 50s, had held two ministries in Cheshire and London, and had also served as an army chaplain. Like his predecessor, he too witnessed apparitions in the church – the first sighting being in August 1945. At first, he remained silent but finally decided to go public in the Acton Gazette in November 1946:

> *Until a few days ago I had not heard of the report of alleged spirit-manifestation in an Acton vicarage in 1938. By the courtesy of the Borough Librarian I have been allowed to read the account, and was*

immediately interested to learn that the ghostly appearance was that of a monk.

About a dozen such monks can be seen on most evenings walking in procession up the centre aisle and into the chancel of St Dunstan's church. They wear golden brown habits and are hooded. Another monk attired in eucharistic vestments occasionally celebrates Mass in the memorial chapel. Four of us, unknown to each other, have witnessed these phenomena, from time to time. We are all truthful folk and it is impossible for four people to suffer from the same hallucination at the same time.

More interesting is a solitary monk, wearing a violet hood, with whom we hold conversation.

The procession of monks probably belonged in some past age to a religious foundation in the locality. They are attracted to the nearest consecrated building. Their deepest satisfaction is to repeat what was their greatest happiness during earth-existence.

My violet-hooded friend belongs to a different class. He is a ministering spirit, sent to inspire and instruct. I am indebted to him, as to many others, for much help.

As you can imagine, this account caused a sensation and soon led to some of his parishioners admitting that they too had seen the monks:

I saw them three or four times on evenings when a discussion group was being held in the vestry. Because of the warm weather, the vestry door leading into the body of the church was kept open, and I saw exactly the same thing on each occasion: a body of monks in brown habits walking in procession up the central aisle towards and into the chancel. Seen out of the corner of the eye they were clear, but disappeared when looked at directly.

I knew nothing of any previous sightings or of the history of the church. The experience had no emotional impact on me – they were just monks walking up the aisle. When I mentioned the occurrence to the vicar he was quite matter of fact about it.

Another newspaper, the Daily Graphic, decided to send a reporter to the church to see if he could discover more about the haunting. The journalist, Kenneth Mason, went there on a cold and wet Friday evening within days of the *Acton Gazette* account being published.

The journalist took up a seat in the far left-hand corner of the nave and settled down for what he expected to be an uneventful night. Cold and wet, he soon drifted off to sleep. He later awoke with a start – he was not sure how long he had been asleep – and was amazed to see six monks in the north aisle, all hooded and with heads bowed.

'Slowly but happily they came towards me. I took my courage in both hands and barred their way. I faced them. Then quickly I had to turn and look back at them. They had passed right through me.'

The monks made for the altar and passed through the reporter two-by-two – 'slightly below my neck and to the left of my collar bone.' He then became aware of a voice addressing him: 'Near here, 500 years ago, stood a monastery. We were its occupants. This is our past, this is our future.'

When they reached the altar the monks started to kneel but at that instant a light at the back of the church came on and someone called out asking who was there. The service bell in the tower started to ring and the monks vanished. Mason looked at his watch and noted that the time was 7.15pm.

The reporter found himself puzzled by what he had seen but remained convinced that he had witnessed something not of this world.

'I cannot explain it,' he later said, 'but I saw these things I saw that night.' The newspaper stood by their reporter and stated that Kenneth Mason was 'a quiet, sober-minded, reliable reporter who has never dabbled in the occult. He was a lieutenant in the Royal Navy during the war.'

That weekend, he returned to the church with a photographer in the hope that they could capture the monks on camera. They saw nothing, but the vicar, Mrs Bonnyfin, his secretary, and a parishioner, Mrs Clare Pembleton, claimed that one of the monks had stood by the vestry door watching the pair as they vainly tried to capture the apparitions on film. The reporter felt that the large number of people attracted to the building that night in the hope of seeing a ghost had somehow 'upset the atmosphere of my previous vigil'.

As you can imagine, the church now became a major attraction for would-be ghost hunters. The vicar was deeply unhappy with this and wrote of his annoyance in the parish magazine:

> *I was rather afraid that the popular Press would vulgarize the manifestations I described, but I was not prepared for the avalanche of letters which reached me from all parts of the world. Apparently every newspaper in the USA published a third-hand account. I was interested to hear from a former Sister here that the curate of her day [Mr Boustead] saw similar phenomena, and from the Psychic Research Society to the effect that they have had St Dunstan's monks on their records for over 12 years. They tell me that the manifestations occur in four-year cycles. As I suspected, more people have witnessed the phenomena than I knew.*

He continued:

> *May I repeat that, apart from the congregations, there are no spirits in the church. These visions are merely thought-pictures, televised by subtle rays, the nature of which are as yet unknown to scientists, but of course somewhere there is a personality responsible, consciously or unconsciously, for the vision. Please dissuade curious sightseers from visiting the church. The whole business is really very trivial and common-place, and was only mentioned as an introduction to the more serious matter of my original article.*

He added:

> *You may be interested to know that the 'radiation' was almost overpowering during the midnight Eucharist.*

The vicar decided to ban further vigils in the church and declined from discussing the monks for several months.

He was later persuaded by a journalist to change his mind but soon came to regret this decision. The January 1948 issue of the parish magazine saw him write about a reporter 'who asked if he might trespass on my valuable time for a chat. He came, and we talked for hours on the most fascinating subject of psychic phenomena, especially as related to religion and philosophy. At times we ascended into the heights of metaphysics and fourth dimensional thought, and both thoroughly enjoyed ourselves.'

The journalist was then shown around the church:

I made one stipulation about anything he might write, and he willingly agreed. It was that the subject should be kept a sacred subject and not be written about lightly or sensationally. Some of you saw last Wednesday's paper and know how horribly the promise was broken. Not one so-called fact is true. There was no owl in the churchyard, no hand on a doorknob, no conversation with the organist, no mention about a 'violet monk' in church last Sunday, no stumbling, and no command from me to be quiet. There was no wind and no strange noises.

Some weeks later an article on confirmation appeared in the parish magazine. It was entitled *Supernatural* and had been dictated – according to the vicar – by the violet-hooded monk. It concerned the Te Deum and suggested how it could be altruistically expressed.

The vicar also revealed that the violet-hooded monk continued to appear on a regular basis and was able to speak with him through his secretary, Mrs Bonnyfin, who possessed mediumistic qualities. He also stated that the monk appeared at confirmation classes and had even promised further contributions to the magazine.

It has to be said that several of the vicar's parishioners were highly sceptical of his claims. Mr F. H. Harris, a churchwarden and voluntary verger, had been in the church on numerous occasions and had seen and heard nothing. But shortly before his death in 1948, he admitted to his wife that the vicar had been right after all – he too had finally witnessed a ghostly monk in the church. He also confirmed this to a local shopkeeper with whom he had been friendly for many years.

A Mr R. N. G. Rowland, the church organist and another former sceptic, also had a few strange experiences in the church:

One Sunday evening after service, I was leaning over the back pew side-by-side with another chorister, discussing music (not a word or thought about ghosts), and we were staring vaguely down the church towards the chancel. The only others in the church were the vicar, the verger and a warden, who were in the vicar's vestry. The nave was fairly well lit, the chancel in darkness. Quite suddenly, for no apparent reason, we stopped talking (we had been having an animated conversation) and stood silent gazing up into the chancel. I was aware of unseen activity there, and in a low voice said to my friend, 'Do you see anything?' He answered 'No, but there's something going on in the chancel.' I said, 'The vicar says that they hold services there.' 'Oh, the monks,' he replied. 'Yes, I believe it now. I didn't before, but I know they're there now.'

On another occasion, the organist was conducting choir practice with an assistant at the organ. The vicar was also present:

We were rehearsing Stanford's And I saw another angel *for All Saints' tide. In one of the more lush, full passages, looking a few bars ahead, I saw a typical 'horn cue' in the organ accompaniment. I said to myself, 'Oh, for an orchestra to do this full justice.' At that moment we reached the 'horn cue' and I distinctly heard the two horns – an effect quite impossible to reproduce on the organ – singing out their parts above everybody else. After we had finished the anthem I said to the vicar, 'Well, if it goes like that on Sunday, we shan't have anything to worry about.' 'Yes, very good,' he replied, 'but you might not have the orchestra with you on Sunday.' 'What orchestra?' I asked, deliberately. 'Come off it,' he said, 'you know as well as I do that you had a full spirit symphony orchestra out there in the chancel, playing along with*

you. Didn't you see them? I did.' 'No,' I replied, 'I did not see them.'
'Ah, but you knew they were there, didn't you?' he said. And somehow
I could not deny it.

In December 1946 the Society for Psychical Research looked into the case. The report compiled by a Mr C.P.O.D. Scott stated that Anton-Stephens had also witnessed the phantasm of another church develop within the present church. This had usually occurred during services. He also confirmed that he had seen ghosts at his former church and was a believer in the theory of spiritualism but disapproved of the practice as it 'artificially encouraged phenomena'. Scott also interviewed Mrs Bonnyfin and Miss Pembleton, who confirmed that they too had seen the apparitions. Mr Scott thought that the vicar was a witness of average reliability. However, he was concerned that the two ladies may have been influenced by Anton-Stephens and his conviction that the church was haunted.

Mr Scott also interviewed Kenneth Mason, the reporter. He repeated his story and stated that the monks had appeared solid with chubby and round faces. He also said that violet-hooded monk had communicated to him in modern English. Mr Mason struck Mr Scott as an 'acute and reliable observer.'

The Rev. Anton-Stephens continued to see the monks and was certain that they followed a four-year cycle. He explained that a build-up of spirit-energy in the church – sometimes lasting 15 months – resulted in an increased number of appearances which then lapsed as the cycle came to an end. The whole cycle would then start anew. Interestingly, the violet-hooded monk did not appear to follow this pattern and could appear at any given time.

For the rest of his time at St Dunstan's, the vicar decided not to publish anything further on the monks. He also continued to actively discourage those seeking to hold vigils in the church. The vicar retired in 1961 and died the following year.

But this was not the end of the story …

Mr Rowland, the organist, had one further strange experience in 1966:

I went into church one evening, about half an hour before the boys' choir practice, to play the organ. The church door was open to allow the boys to enter as they arrived. After playing for some ten minutes I felt a movement behind me, as if someone had stepped into the choir-stall and was standing behind my left shoulder. For a split second I assumed that one of the boys had arrived early, and I looked over my shoulder. There was no one to be seen – but there was certainly someone standing there. I had not stopped playing, and I just carried on, projecting a thought of 'Good evening – it's nice of you to come and listen to me.' I had no sense of fear or discomfort, rather a sense of elation. And until a boy came in a few minutes later, and broke the spell, I know that whoever was standing there was emanating a feeling of pleasure and approval, and wanting me to go on playing because he was enjoying it so much.

It later emerged that his son had an identical sensation when playing the organ.

Peter Underwood investigated the haunting and interviewed several of the witnesses to the phenomena. One parishioner told him that on several occasions he had visited the church in the evening and been confronted by a procession of monks moving through the church towards the chancel. He also discovered that unconfirmed sightings of the monks dated back to the 1920s.

Another parishioner, a Mrs Alma Baker, told him how she used to arrange flowers in the church and often felt an overwhelming impression that she was being watched, although she never actually witnessed the monks herself. Sometimes the feeling was so strong that she was compelled to leave the building for a few minutes.

To say that the haunting of St Dunstan's is one of the most interesting cases on record would certainly be an understatement. Over the years several parishioners – including those formally sceptical of the phenomena – saw or felt the presence of several monks in the church. And let us not forget that both the Rev. Anton-Stephens and Kenneth Mason also claimed to have been in communication with one of the ghostly figures. Clearly, this is more than just a case of auto-suggestion, misidentification or hoax.

The Rev. Anton-Stephens was always convinced that the monks had been unable to move on and were drawn to St Dunstan's because it was the nearest existing consecrated building to their former place of worship.

St Dunstan's still stands but the church authorities appear less than keen to discuss the subject of ghosts as the building is still used as a place of worship. Rumours persist that the monks still walk but confirmation of this from eye witnesses has proved lacking.

So have the phantom monks and their mysterious violet-hooded leader finally moved on from this world to another plane of existence? Only time will tell.

Chapter 10

THE GREEN LADY OF FYVIE CASTLE AND OTHER HAUNTING TALES

F yvie Castle can be found to the north west of Aberdeen. The current building traces its origins back to the 13th century and is now in the care of the National Trust for Scotland following its sale in 1982.

Like many a Scottish castle, it can lay claim to several interesting tales of the supernatural, including ghosts, a sealed room, curses and even a weeping stone.

The ghost who signed its name

At the start of the 17th century Fyvie was owned by Alexander Seton, later the Earl of Dunfermline and Lord Chancellor of Scotland. In 1590 he married Dame Lilias Drummond, who was the daughter of Patrick Drummond, a member of Scottish nobility. They had five daughters together but tragedy struck the couple in May 1601 when Dame Lilias suddenly died at the age of 27.

The official story is that the couple were happily married. But were they? Rumour has it that Seton was deeply unhappy that his wife had failed to provide him with a male heir and so embarked on an affair with Lady Grizel Leslie, his step-niece and the daughter of James Leslie, Master of Rothes. Dame Lilias learned of her husband's infidelity and soon died of a broken heart. Others, however, claimed that she had been murdered in order to make way for Lady Grizel. Seton was accused of sealing his wife in a small room in one of the castle's towers and slowly starving her to death.

The fact that Seton was to marry Lady Grizel less than six months after Dame Drummond's death hardly suggests a grieving widower. Indeed,

Fyvie Castle. (public domain)

he proposed within a few weeks of his wife's demise. So was the tale of murder true after all?

On the night of 27 October 1601, Seton and his new bride retired to a bedroom in the castle. Their new bedchamber had not yet been completed and the couple were forced to use a small room in the older part of the building. Their wedding night was not to be an enjoyable one as they were disturbed by strange human-like sighs from just outside their bedroom window, a window that was over 50 feet from the ground. Seton looked out of the room but could see nothing.

In the morning, Seton and his wife awoke from a troubled sleep and went to the window. They were shocked to see carved on the windowsill the name 'D. LILES DRUMMOND'.

The letters, some three inches high, were neatly carved and faced outwards from the castle – you can still see them to this day. It was later suggested that the name had been carved by a disgruntled member of Seton's staff who had been disgusted by his master's treatment of his first wife. However, there were no footholds in the wall and the 50 foot drop would have proved a formidable obstacle to any would-be hoaxer. The couple had only chosen the room at short notice and the noise of someone carving neat and deep cut letters into the stone right outside their room would have hardly gone unnoticed by Seton or his bride.

The mystery of the writing was never explained, but soon after the castle began to be haunted by a Green Lady which many came to suspect was the spirit of Dame Lilias. The figure was usually described as having a greenish glow about her and mainly confined herself to the spiral staircase and corridor close to the bedroom where the mysterious carving had first appeared. The apparition was also often accompanied by the smell of roses.

Colonel Cosmo Gordon who owned the castle in the 19th century spoke of having once been shaken out of bed by an invisible assailant. On another occasion a wind inside the castle – when the surrounding countryside was calm – blew off his bedsheets and those of his guests. He assumed that the Green Lady was responsible. Gordon came to regard her as having a special connection with his family and once wrote of a guest who had stayed at the castle with her maid. One morning, she told Cosmo that her maid had seen a lady in a green dress walking up the main staircase of the castle. Gordon explained that it must have been the ghost of the Green Lady but was puzzled as the phantom was only supposed to appear to a member of the Gordon family. The lady then revealed that her maid's name was Gordon.

The Green Lady was seen just before Cosmo's death in 1879. He described how she appeared to be beckoning to him. His younger brother also saw the apparition a few days later. She walked towards him, paused and then made a slow curtsey before vanishing. Cosmo died the next day.

During the Great War a Canadian army officer visited Fyvie. He was a non-believer when it came to ghosts but soon changed his mind after witnessing unexplained phenomena there. Upon retiring to bed, he found that his room was illuminated by a strange light – described by him as being like 'little flames playing around the pictures' – which grew steadily brighter as he watched. This occurred every night during his stay and, although the Green Lady failed to appear, the officer described feeling a presence in the room which he strangely felt hatred for.

In 1920 the castle was owned by the Leiths. During that year an unpleasant fungus was found growing on the wall of the gun room. The laird called in workmen and during the removal of a wall they found a human skeleton. This discovery coincided with an increase in appearances of the Green Lady. A maid described how she saw a 'white object' emerge from the wall of her bedroom. She realised that the object was in fact a woman dressed in a whitish-green gown. The figure then 'sailed' across the room and appeared to be aware of the maid as she looked at her sadly before drifting through a closed door. Others at the castle also saw the figure passing through walls and the laird decided to return the skeleton to the place where it had been found.

However, some claim that the skeleton has nothing to do with the Green Lady. It has been suggested that the bones are the mortal remains of Lady Meldrum, who in the 1400s apparently requested that her remains be interred in the castle walls. She is also supposed to walk Fyvie from time to time and has become known as the Grey Lady in order to avoid confusion with her green namesake!

In 1995 the actor Robert Hardy travelled to Fyvie to film a documentary on the ghosts of the castle. He spoke to Major John Payton, the curator of arms and armour, who confirmed that he had seen the Green Lady in January 1992. He had been in the drawing room when he stepped aside to allow a woman to pass him. When he looked again, the figure had gone. All that was left was the smell of rose perfume. The major spoke with staff members to see if anyone else had been in that part of the castle but found that he had been completely alone at the time of his encounter.

A month later, the major found himself having to comfort a distressed tourist. The lady had been in one of the bedrooms and had been looking into a mirror. She had been shocked to see another woman looking back at her. The figure had been surrounded by a haze of shimmering green and was described as wearing a long, full-length dress with a string of pearls around her neck.

A dressing room off the Gordon bedroom continues to remain unnaturally cold and now appears to be the favoured haunt of the Green Lady. In July 2002 an Australian tourist saw her here and staff often report the feeling of being watched in this part of the castle.

The sealed chamber

Beneath the Charter Room is a sealed chamber which legend claims should never be opened. Any attempt to do so will result in the death of the owner of the castle or blindness for his wife. Two lairds ignored this warning and paid the price for their folly. In 1816 General William Gordon attempted unsuccessfully to locate the room. He died suddenly and his wife, a former domestic servant, went blind. Sixty years later, another Gordon, Sir Maurice, also decided to find the chamber. On the very day that his men started work, Sir Maurice fell and broke his leg. He immediately called a halt to the job and assumed that he had evaded the curse. He was to be sadly disappointed as shortly after his wife developed a painful condition of the eyes which was to affect her for the rest of her life.

The weeping stone

In the 13th century the owner of Fyvie had the misfortune to upset a famous psychic and poet of the day, Thomas the Rhymer, who had made it known he intended to visit the castle. It was ordered that the castle's main door should remain open but Thomas, never one to rush things, took seven years and a day to make good his promise. As luck would have it, a storm blew up as he neared the castle entrance and the door slammed shut in his face. Thomas was furious and uttered a curse upon the castle and its inhabitants:

Fyvie, Fyvie, thou's never thrive
As lang's there's in thee stanes (stones) three

There's ane intill (one in) the oldest tower

There's ane intill the ladye's bower

There's ane intill the water-yett (water gate)

And thir three stanes ye never get.

Although it was never mentioned in the rhyme, it was believed that Thomas had also declared that no first born would inherit the castle until the stones – boundary markers removed from a nearby religious building – had been found. One of the stones was eventually recovered but the others remain lost to this day.

It may appear that this centuries-old curse is simply the stuff of legend but it is strange to relate that no direct male heir of Fyvie ever succeeded to the estate up to its sale to the National Trust in 1982. The stone is still kept in the castle and is known as 'the weeping stone' due to the fact that it can become suddenly wet. There is no mystery in this as scientific examination of the stone has revealed it to be porous sandstone and it is therefore able to absorb and exude moisture from the air. Despite this, the stone does have a somewhat sinister reputation. Christopher Hartley, a senior member of the castle staff, had been working on conservation of the stone prior to its public display. He found that contact with it coincided with several mishaps ranging from twisting his ankle and spraining his knee to suddenly being rushed to hospital with kidney stones. He quickly came to regard the stone as being responsible for these misfortunes and from that moment on decided to give it a wide berth.

The trumpeter

Another ghost at Fyvie is that of Andrew Lammie, an 18th century trumpeter who fell madly in love with Agnes Smith, a miller's daughter. Unfortunately, his rival in love was Gordon, the Laird of Fyvie. He 'arranged' for Andrew to be seized and transported to the West Indies. After several years Andrew managed to escape and returned to Scotland where he learned that Agnes had died of a broken heart. The shock killed the trumpeter, but not before he cursed the laird, promising that he would return to blow his trumpet upon the death of every future owner of Fyvie. Since then, a figure wearing tartan has been seen in the castle grounds. And, as expected, the sounds of a trumpet were also heard prior to the death of a laird for many years afterwards.

Fyvie has a strange atmosphere to it and, once inside, you cannot help sensing the presence of the castle's former inhabitants. It is little wonder that one member of the castle's staff has gone on record as saying that, 'the air here is very busy with more than human visitors'.

Chapter 11

SHADOWS OF EVIL

Can spirits bring psychical harm to the living? Experience has sadly taught me that not all hauntings can be classed as harmless. I have come across several cases where the spirit actually seems to take a positive delight in generating fear and terror in all those who encounter it. Some properties even seem to possess a malevolent aura – something that can bring misfortune to those unfortunate enough to stay there. I know of one Victorian property that seems to possess an 'unlucky' nature. Businesses never prosper there and two of the more recent owners died in a car accident shortly after leaving the building. For years it stood empty before it was rented again. One can only wonder if the 'curse' – if such a word is appropriate – will ever be lifted and peace finally restored to the building?

So what is the truth behind such hauntings? Is it simply a case of an evil person continuing their evil beyond death? Or can a violent and terrible event somehow leave a malevolent field which then affects all those who unwittingly enter it? Or are we dealing with a type of elemental, an entity that needs to feed on fear in order to survive?

Read on and decide for yourself ...

A victim's curse?

James Wentworth Day was a noted writer and broadcaster of the 20th century. He published a large number of books and articles on subjects ranging from the history of East Anglia to biographies of Sir Malcolm Campbell and the Queen Mother's family. He also wrote several studies of the paranormal and is still fondly remembered today by many in the field as one of the first modern ghost hunters.

In the mid-1930s Day decided to take a lease on 2 King Street in London, a pleasant looking house which dated back to the reign of Charles

II. Surprisingly, the rent was only £225 a year, including the rates. He was later to wonder if the owners – The Crown – were aware of the building's history and had leased him a curse rather than a bargain.

Day's flat was on the third and fourth floors and consisted of a sitting/dining room, three bedrooms, dressing room, kitchen and bathroom. At the time he was the editor of the Illustrated Sporting and Dramatic News and asked his assistant editor, Lieut.-Cdr. Peter Kemp RN, if he would like to share the flat as he felt it was too big for one man. Kemp agreed and took the upper floor for his own use.

On the day they moved in, Day was alone in his bedroom while his companion unpacked his belongings upstairs. Day suddenly felt a sense of dread and became aware that something was staring at him from the fireplace in the left-hand corner of the room. His companion was less than sympathetic upon hearing this and dismissed these feelings at 'rot'. However, Day was not so sure. It seemed to him that the house possessed an intangible presence, a certain something which seemed ill-disposed to both him and his colleague.

Things started to go badly for Day after moving in. He lost his job and then his flat mate suddenly announced that he was leaving to live in the country. Day contacted another friend, a certain Gordon Dickson, who agreed to move in and share the expense of running the property. It was not long before he too became aware of the malevolent presence and left. He tragically died in a car crash shortly after moving out.

Day then married. The marriage proved a failure. Things continued to go from bad to worse. His father-in-law committed suicide and his beloved Scots housekeeper moved out. Day was now left alone in the house – a house which he had come to hate.

He asked two young friends to keep him company. They were the daughter and son of a friend who owned an estate in Ireland.

One Saturday night, Day returned from a shooting trip when heard a scream from upstairs. 'Uncle James, please come up quickly! I'm so frightened!' Day rushed up the stairs to find the girl in a state of shock. After calming her down, he managed to find out what had happened. She had not been aware that he had gone out and had decided to pop down to the sitting room for a chat. Looking through the half-open door into his bedroom, she had seen a man in the left-hand corner of the room. He was sitting in a chair and was bound hand and foot. His eyes were protruding horribly and his tongue was hanging out of his mouth. He had been strangled. A search by Day revealed nothing to account for the appearance of the apparition. It was hardly surprising that after this he gave up the flat and moved out.

Day later learned that subsequent tenants also suffered misfortune. One, an ex-officer, died in debt after his business failed. Finally, an art dealer took the house and installed his sister there, filling the house with valuable paintings and furniture.

One night, Day found himself walking through St James's with a Canadian friend. The man prided himself on a thorough knowledge of the area and upon reaching 2 King's Street he pointed towards the house with his cane: 'That, gentlemen, is the unluckiest house in St James's. Everybody who has lived there has had bad luck – bankrupt, hurt in accidents, killed in car crashes or just plain miserable.'

Day asked him why this should be so. His guide then explained that in 1810 the Duke of Cumberland, son of George III, was widely thought to have murdered his manservant in St James's Palace. The man's name was Sellis and it was believed that Cumberland had seduced the man's daughter. She had become pregnant and had committed suicide. Sellis had discovered the truth and was killed by the Duke during a violent scuffle in the man's bedroom.

Cumberland denied this and claimed that he had been attacked in his own chambers by Sellis. The manservant had then fled to his own rooms and cut his throat. Few believed this as the razor used in the supposed suicide was found on the other side of the man's bedroom – too far to have been thrown there by Sellis in such a condition. However, the authorities were less inclined to challenge the Duke's version of events and the matter was dropped.

Unfortunately for the Duke, a valet had seen him fleeing Sellis's room on the night of the murder. The Duke heard of this and got the man assigned to a German officer who lived at No 2 King Street. Upon arriving there, the valet was tied to a chair and garrotted.

'They say his ghost still appears – eyes staring and tongue sticking out. His curse is on that house, gentlemen!'

Day then admitted to the Canadian that he had lived there also. The man looked at him sharply and replied, 'You got out just in time, sir.'

And what of the house today? It was destroyed during the Second World War. A German bomb hit the building, instantly killing the sister of the art dealer and reducing the house and antiques to ash and rubble. How ironic that it fell to Adolf Hitler and the weapons of war to finally lay the curse of King Street.

Thora Hird and the haunted jacket

The Duke of York's Theatre in St Martin's Lane was once home to an article of clothing known as the 'Strangler Jacket' and the late Dame Thora Hird was just one of the many people to be strangely affected when wearing it.

The year was 1948 and Thora Hird was appearing as the leading lady in *A Queen Came By*, a production set during Queen Victoria's Jubilee. The play had opened at the Embassy Theatre in Swiss Cottage and a search through a trunk of old clothes in the attic produced a jacket which seemed perfect for Miss Hird's role as a seamstress.

The garment in question, a short-backed, bolero-style jacket in embroidered velvet (also known as a monkey jacket), was part of the theatre's store of old costumes and dated from the 1890s. No one was really sure where it had originally come from. Some claimed it had been made for

Thora Hird experienced feelings of distress when wearing the jacket. (public domain)

an early production of *Charley's Aunt*, while others maintained that it had been bought from a second-hand clothes stall in a London market.

Although the size was right and appeared roomy, the actress soon complained of tightness around the chest and arms. The jacket was let out but it still seemed to get tighter every time she wore it. A cameo brooch, part of the jacket, also seemed to sticking into her throat and was removed from the jacket when they took the play to the Duke of York's Theatre.

Things then seemed to go from bad to worse. 'I never really liked the feel of that jacket', Miss Hird later recalled. 'It felt strange. There was an unpleasant sensation of tightness. I was never comfortable in it. And then there was one day when I was away filming and my understudy Erica Foyle had to take my place. She was very psychic and wearing that jacket affected her even more than it did me.

'She didn't know about the experiences I had had, but she experienced something more. That night, at home in the bathroom of her flat in Sherlock Mews, she saw the figure of a young woman wearing Victorian clothes and the same monkey jacket. Next day at the theatre she said the jacket was evil and implored me not to wear it. "It's evil, very evil." she kept on saying.'

Erica complained about the jacket to the stage manager, Majorie Page, who was then made aware of Thora Hird's experiences with it. She decided to try it on for herself and discovered that it also gave her the same unpleasant feeling around the chest and arms. Mary Pifford, wife of the play's director, also decided to try on the jacket but experienced no ill feelings. However, when she took it off, she found a number of red marks on her throat which to those present appeared consistent with an attempt at strangulation.

It was then decided to remove the jacket from the theatre. Thora Hird wore a cape on stage for the next performance but during the interval Erica Foyle went to the bar and suddenly felt that the jacket was still in the theatre. It was. It had been hidden under the bar, ready to taken away that night.

Frederick Pifford, the play's director, decided to approach a publication, Psychic News, for advice and was advised by the editor, Fred Archer, to allow him to organise a seance on the stage of the theatre in an attempt to discover the reason for the jacket's adverse effects on those who wore it.

The seance was held on the evening of 4 May 1949 with the cast, the stage manager, the director, his wife, the editor of Psychic News and three mediums in attendance. An invited audience of reporters and photographers filled the first three rows.

Fred Archer wrote of the night in his book *Ghost Writer*:

The mediums had been told nothing of the events leading up to the seance. Each in turn was given the jacket to psychometise. The first medium was unable to obtain any distinct psychic impressions. The second said he had the feeling that it had originally belonged to a young woman, but could say nothing further than that.

The coat was then handed to the third medium. He held it for a few moments and then began to describe a dramatic vision. There was a young girl, he said, about 18 to 20 years of age. She had a sense of guilt about something. In some way she had provoked anger akin to madness in a man who, nevertheless, was not essentially evil. The medium said he could see a pair of hands, the rough hands of a workman, tearing at the girl's clothing. The two struggled violently until suddenly the girl fell backwards and there was a splashing as she was forced into a butt of water.

The assailant then dragged her body from the water and carried it up a flight of stairs into a room, squalid and bare save for two pieces of furniture. Then he wrapped the body in a blanket, then carried it downstairs again, still wet and dripping. At that point the vision faded.

It was at this point that Marjorie Page, who was watching all this, then admitted that she too had had a similar vision when wearing the jacket but had kept quiet as the vision had seemed so fantastic.

It was then decided to end the seance with some of the reporters departing. Those who were left, including Fred Archer, made their way to Thora Hird's dressing room where it was agreed to carry on the experiment in quieter conditions.

One reporter, Monica Pearson, wrote of what happened next in an article originally published in the *Reynolds News*:

I don't pretend to be able to explain the strange happenings at the Duke of York's theatre. I simply record what I saw and found rather terrifying. It was unquestionably honest and above board.

The wife of a member of the company, Mrs Mary Piffard, donned the jacket, and sat back in an armchair. Soon she began to look ill, was gasping for breath, clutching at the air, crying: 'Don't touch my throat.'

Another member of the cast tried on the coat. Nothing happened. A third person put on the jacket and was soon gasping for breath, looking very white and in a semi-conscious condition. Again the jacket was hurriedly removed and the victim was revived with water.

Fred Archer then decided that fresh minds were needed as he was worried that suggestion and the excitement of the seance may well be playing a part in the feelings generated by those donning the jacket. He, along with a reporter, left the theatre and searched for likely candidates who would have no prior knowledge of the seance or the jacket. It was well past midnight when the pair spotted a young couple in Trafalgar Square. Fred explained to them that they were newspapermen working on a story and would they be willing to join them in an experiment? Both agreed and the four made their way back to the theatre and Thora Hird's dressing room. It must be stressed at this point that at no time were the couple made aware of the jacket's history or the events connected with it. The slightly perplexed girl tried on the jacket but felt nothing. Her boyfriend, Edward Fosbrook, was then asked to touch the sleeve of the jacket. Fred Archer later recalled what happened:

He put his right hand on the girl's arm. As he did so a queer expression crossed his face. Asked what was wrong, he said he had the feeling of wanting to grip the arm tightly. He placed his left hand on the other sleeve of the jacket, then moved both hands higher. The nearer they came to the girl's throat, he said, the more the impulse grew upon him. Suddenly he wrenched himself away, dropping his arms to his sides.

*It appeared that the boy, rather than the girl, might possess some
kind of sensitive powers. When she took off the jacket we asked him if he
would wear it. Amid mounting tension he put it on.*

*Straightaway he appeared to be having difficulty with his breathing.
After a few moments he gasped out: 'There is something sinister – like
death. It feels as if someone were trying to kill me. But in a just way.'*

The young man then took off the jacket and Fred asked why he had
used the words 'in a just way'. The man said that he had no idea but Fred
then recalled the medium who had said that the murdered woman had
felt a sense of guilt on the night of her death. So was the young man also
picking up the thoughts of her attacker, a man who had felt justified in
killing the unfortunate girl?

The jacket was removed from the theatre and sold to a man by the
name of Lloyd who lived in Los Angeles. His wife tried on the jacket and
found herself exhausted with a feeling of suffocation and a pressure on
her legs. A 16-year-old girl also tried it on and described how she felt as
though fingers were grabbing her throat. Two other woman also tried on
the jacket and both experienced similar feelings.

So what are we to make of all this? Sceptics claim that the whole
business was nothing more than a case of mass hysteria caused by an
ill-fitting jacket and superstitious actors. But what of the apparition seen
by Erica Foyle or the experiences of the young man brought in on the
night of the seance, a person who had no prior knowledge of the sinister
feelings connected with the jacket?

Thora Hird was later told it had originally been worn by a girl named
Edith Merryweather who had been wearing it on the night of her death
at the hands of a jealous boyfriend.

So was the jacket worn by a young woman on the day of her murder?
And did the murderous feelings of her attacker combined with the
terror of the girl somehow imprint themselves into the very fabric of the
garment?

No one seems to know what subsequently became of the jacket after it was sold to Mr Lloyd.

A study in terror

The year was 1971 and Joy McKenna was living in the village of Broadway in Worcestershire. Her husband often made early-morning business trips and so slept in one of the spare rooms in order to avoid disturbing his wife. Despite this, Joy would usually set her alarm clock to coincide with his so she could cook him breakfast and see him off.

One night in November, Mrs McKenna retired to bed at 11pm. She set her alarm for 6.30am and was soon fast asleep.

She awoke sometime later and assumed that it was morning. She was rather annoyed as she still felt tired and was somewhat reluctant to leave the warmth of her bed. Suddenly, she was seized with a strange feeling of apprehension. It seemed that something was in the bedroom with her – and whatever it was slowly moving alongside the bed! She thought for a moment that it was her husband but this belief was soon shattered when she suddenly became aware of his snores in the next room.

The sense of fear became overpowering and she ducked under the bedclothes in an attempt to hide from whatever or whoever was in the room with her. It did her little good. In an instant, the entity leapt onto the bed and started to hit her about the chest, shoulders and arms. Mrs McKenna felt that she was being crushed under an immense weight and tried to scream out for help. She found that she was unable to do so – her vocal cords and body were paralysed.

Although it was dark, she could clearly see two large amber eyes staring at her through the bedclothes. The sense of evil was now overwhelming. She began to pray, pleading to God to release her from the clutches of whatever was upon her. As if in reaction to this, the creature suddenly slithered away from her and dropped to the floor. She was now able to scream, throwing herself from the bed and praying like never before. Her husband, now awoken by her shouts, rushed in to see what was wrong.

At first, her husband thought that she had suffered a nightmare but finally became convinced that what his wife had experienced was no dream. It was then recalled that she had witnessed a strange incident only two days before.

The couple had four cats and would often allow the animals to sleep on the beds. His wife had gone to the bedroom – the same one where she had been attacked – and had noticed a lump under the covers. She assumed it was one of the cats but became puzzled when it slithered – never once changing its shape – over the side of the bed and vanished without trace. She returned downstairs and was surprised to discover all four cats locked in the dining room.

The reason for the attack on Mrs McKenna was never explained. Nor did the house – built in the 1930s – have a reputation for being haunted. The entity never appeared again.

The creature on the stairs

The following case has never been published before. The name of the person and the location of the house have been withheld at their request.

The house where I lived dated from the 1950s and had been built on the site of an earlier Victorian building. I shared my home with a pet dog and spent my time writing and touring the county in search of material for my books. One night in 1990, I can't remember the exact date, I retired to bed and soon found myself sound asleep. At some point in the night I awoke with a sense that something was about to happen. Suddenly, I became aware of something running up the stairs at tremendous speed. It burst through the door into my room and began to run around my bed, darting backwards and forwards, almost as if deciding what to do next. I hid under the bedclothes and waited in fear to see what would happen. I felt instinctively that the entity was a large dog, almost wolf-like, and was wholly malevolent. I also knew that to look at it would be fateful for me. Suddenly and without warning it disappeared .

After several minutes, I managed to pluck up the courage to leave my bed and turn on the light. The door was firmly closed and a search of the house revealed nothing. My dog was apparently undisturbed and lay fast asleep in the spare room.

The events of that night were repeated many times over the next ten years. Sometimes several months would go by before 'it' put in another appearance. The pattern was always the same – the stairs, the door, the bed and then silence. It even followed me when I moved. Any thoughts that my own dog was somehow responsible for the events will be dispelled when you learn that the visits continued long after he died.

It may surprise you to discover that over the years I became rather unconcerned by the nocturnal visits – fear had been replaced by a reluctant acceptance of the creature. The time between appearances gradually became longer and longer and finally they stopped altogether. It's now been ten years since the entity last appeared.

Why did it start to haunt me? Why did it apparently bare me ill-will? And why did it finally leave? These are questions that I still ponder to this day.

Chapter 12

THE CRAWLING LADY OF ARDACHIE

One of Scotland's strangest tales of the paranormal concerns Ardachie, a 19th-century shooting lodge, which overlooked Loch Ness near Fort Augustus.

Ardachie (Gaelic for High Field) consisted of a main house, a game-keeper's cottage, a shepherd's house, walled garden, two arable fields and some 1,700 acres of hill land. The property had been owned by a Mrs Lily Bruen since 1924. She died in the early 1950s, her son deciding to sell the property as he had no interest in maintaining it.

The entire estate was put on the market and in December 1952 it was bought by Peter McEwan, a qualified psychologist. His wife, Dorothy, was a university graduate and they had two young children. The couple had been living in London since their marriage but had decided to look for a new home in order to raise livestock. They planned to breed pigs and the Ardachie estate appeared perfect for this.

The McEwans soon added more animals to their livestock and it was decided to advertise for a live-in couple to help look after the main house, their two children and the animals.

An advert was placed in a London newsagents by Peter McEwan's mother. The interviews were conducted in London with none of those interviewed being told of the couple's identity or the location of the property. A Mr and Mrs McDonald were eventually picked. The husband, Bill, was in his 40s and had been a postman and millwright. Leaving his job as a postman meant that he would lose his pension but he was keen to start a new life with his wife, Frances. She was half French and half Scottish, roughly the same age as her husband

and had been previously employed as a housekeeper in London. Both were originally from Edinburgh and were keen to quit London as it was thought that leaving its polluted air would improve Mrs McDonald's health.

17 August 1953 saw the couple arrive by train. They were met at Spean Bridge station by Peter McEwan's father who occasionally stayed in the game-keeper's cottage on the estate. The McDonalds were both tired after their long journey and, after making an inspection of the grounds and house, retired early to their rooms.

Mr and Mrs McEwan and their father-in-law settled down for supper but at 10.30pm they were somewhat surprised to find the McDonalds burst in and asked if there was anything 'wrong' with their room. They then enquired if any person had come up the stairs. The McEwans confirmed that no one had.

Mrs McDonald explained that after retiring to bed, footsteps had been heard coming up the stairs and along the corridor outside their room. The steps then appeared to enter the empty room opposite theirs. A few minutes later the footsteps were heard again and Frances awakened her husband in some alarm. He listened and thought that the footsteps were coming from behind the wall near the bed and not the corridor.

The McEwans explained that it could have been their dog, cat or even the hum of the generator. The McDonalds rejected all these explanations.

All the household now retired to bed but some 20 minutes later the McDonalds again disturbed the McEwans. They looked terrified. They had heard several loud raps on the wall adjoining the corridor. The rapping had ceased the moment the light had been turned on.

They all gathered in the kitchen and it was decided that Peter McEwan and Bill McDonald would return to the bedroom. They waited in the dark for 15 minutes but nothing happened.

It was decided to move the McDonalds to a guest room. It was separated from their old room by two flights of stairs and a corridor.

Upon entering the room, Frances McDonald crossed to the far wall and listened intently at the fireplace. She then exclaimed, 'She's in here. There's a woman in the room.' She turned and looked transfixed into the corner of the room. Dorothy McEwan, alarmed, snapped at her, 'Don't look like that ...'

Frances seemed to be in a trance and it was a minute or more before she came out of it. She explained that she had heard a sound like the swishing of wings. Then she saw 'an old lady with a cap on her head, a shawl around her shoulders and a hand in front of (and hiding) her face, beckoning me to follow her. She had straggling grey hair which looked as if it had been curly in her younger days.'

Peter McEwan asked Frances if she had felt anything when looking over the house and grounds earlier that day. She recalled feeling revulsion after being strangely compelled to enter a small overgrown garden which lay below the study window.

It was decided to move the couple to another part of the house, a room opposite the McEwans's own bedroom. The doors were left open and the lights were kept on. It was not long before the McDonalds were again disturbed by a rapping sound above their heads. As they all stood in the corridor, Frances again claimed to see the figure of the old woman: 'There she is again. Can't you see her? Now she is crawling on her hands and knees with what looks like a candle stick in one hand. She is outside that room,' she said, pointing to a bathroom.

Peter McEwan asked her to address the figure and Frances asked, 'What's troubling you?' The figure did not respond. Frances, in a state of distress, then said that the woman had crawled round the corner at the end of the corridor but had then crawled back towards them. None of the others could see the phantom. This proved too much for the housekeeper and she had to be helped downstairs to the kitchen. It was decided to move all of the household for the night to the game-keeper's cottage on the estate.

Peter McEwan decided to look into the matter and that same morning visited their nearest neighbour, a Mrs Beckett, who had been a close friend of the former owners, the Bruens.

Mrs Beckett confirmed that Lily Bruen had spent her last years suffering from terrible arthritis and the onset of dementia. She later had a stroke and used to crawl about her home on her hands and knees, holding a candle, convinced that her jewellery had been stolen by the servants. She had also spent a lot of time in Ardachie's rose garden and one night had been found crawling around it in the dark. Mrs Beckett had been obliged to rescue her. She went on to explain that Mrs Bruen had been removed to an Inverness nursing home where she had died around 1950. She confirmed that Mrs McDonald's description of the ghost matched that of her friend. She had indeed worn a small red hat and a kind of shawl.

Peter McEwan was a member of the Society for Psychical Research and it was at this point that he decided to ring them about Ardachie and Mrs McDonald's experiences there. They agreed to send two investigators to look into the matter.

Peter McEwan returned to the house and wondered what would happen next. Nothing occurred during the day and at 9.30pm the McDonalds moved their beds into the small kitchen. At 9.45pm Frances suddenly remembered that she had not brought in the milk which was left every evening on the hall table by a local shepherd. She approached the door and, as she did so, heard rapping sounds from the other side. She opened it and found herself facing the same elderly woman that she had seen before. She was at the bottom of the stairs, her features were indistinct and she appeared wraith-like. Mrs McDonald slammed the door shut and ran back to the kitchen.

The third and fourth nights were again unpleasant for the McDonalds as they continued to hear raps and knocks after they had retired for the night. These sounds continued even after the lights had been turned on.

The 21st saw two members of the SPR, Mr J. D. Matheson, a young teacher and sceptic, and Mr R. Ross OBE, a retired diplomat and a believer in the paranormal, arrive at Ardachie.

Ross and Mathelson were left alone with the Mcdonalds and both thought that Frances seemed 'unnaturally' willing to co-operate with the investigation. She told them that she had even returned to the rose garden that same evening to see if the elderly woman would appear but had seen nothing.

At 10.30pm the household, including the two members of the SPR, gathered in the kitchen where the McDonalds were now sleeping. The lights were switched off with only the glow from the cooker left to illuminate the room. Raps were again heard apparently coming from the window wall and the sound – usually in threes – was likened to knuckles rapping on wood. It was noted that Frances would sigh at the same time as the raps.

Mr Ross watched Mrs McDonald and later reported to the SPR that 'She appeared to become transfixed. A lit cigarette dropped from her right hand on to the carpet. Her two arms hung rigid by her side. Her attention was focussed, glassily, on the open door.'

Mrs McDonald then screamed and the lights were turned on. She said that she had seen a 'younger woman' come into the room. No one else had seen her. Frances claimed that her pulse was racing but Matheson, upon checking it, found it normal.

It was decided to let her rest in bed, her husband staying with her. The investigators then returned after being summoned by Bill McDonald as more raps had been heard after the lights had been turned off. Frances was noted to be breathing with some difficulty. She suddenly sat up and asked her husband if she had been dreaming. She then began to talk about a neglected rose tree and mentioned that 'someone has moved a rose tree.'

Her words struck a chord with the McEwans. When they had first arrived at Ardachie, Peter had looked at the greenhouse and decided to transfer a rose tree growing there to the outside where it died. It later emerged from Mrs Beckett, the neighbour, that the rose tree had been Lily Bruen's favourite.

Mrs McDonald had not been aware of this. Indeed, she had not spoken to the neighbours or even the gardener who had originally been asked to remove the tree.

It was noticed that Frances's right hand lay under the bedclothes and Mr Matheson wondered if she was causing the sounds herself. He decided to shine a torch on the wall where the sounds had originated. He failed to detect any movement from her but she then became upset and it was decided to bring the session to an end.

Matheson and Ross decided to sleep in the bedroom where the McDonalds had first heard the rapping sounds but experienced nothing. They returned to London the next day but not before Frances revealed to them that the apparition of the younger woman she had seen the previous day had been the image of Mrs McEwan. She had not revealed this at the time as it could have upset the couple.

The 22nd saw Peter McEwan determined to find the source of the rapping sounds. He called on the couple unannounced. Nothing occurred and he suggested that she retire to bed in order to rest. The lights were turned off and the sounds suddenly started up again. Peter asked the husband to hold his wife's hands. The raps continued but now appeared to come from the area of her knees.

The housekeeper twice jumped out of the bed after claiming that she had seen a shadow move or that something had pressed down on the bed. This coincided with Peter McEwan trying to get nearer to the source of the rapping sounds. This naturally made him suspicious and he wrote to the SPR that, 'The impression was forced on me that the disturbance(s) had been designed (deliberately?) to withdraw my attention from what Mrs McDonald consciously or unconsciously believed I might have seen.'

The McEwans did not confront the housekeeper and then decided to take a break from the main house. Frances claimed that after they had left two loud raps had been heard on the door. She felt that it was the spirit saying goodbye. Had the housekeeper realised McEwan's suspicions and lied about the goodbye message in order to explain why nothing more was heard from the spirit?

The McEwans decided to let the couple go and, a mere 12 days after they had arrived, Frances and her husband found themselves back on a train to London.

Before they departed, the mattresses in the room where the couple had stayed were changed and a friend of the McEwans saw Frances remove a square box or book from beneath. Under the husband's bed was also an object that looked like a pair of bellows. Had these been used to make the rapping sounds?

Had the housekeeper been faking it all along? After all, only she had seen the figures and the raps were always around her. She also claimed to be psychic and took pride in the fact. She came from a family where her stepmother hated her. She also had two failed marriages behind her. Frances was also described as over-excitable and it cannot be ruled out that she faked the phenomena in order to gain attention. But it should also be noted that neither Frances nor Bill sought publicity in the newspapers after they left Ardachie – it later emerged that the couple were not really married. Indeed, Bill was being pursued for back payments of alimony.

Peter McEwan was convinced that the raps had been caused by the housekeeper's body but without 'her conscious knowledge'.

But how had she heard about the rose tree and the fact that Lily Bruen used to crawl around the main house? She had not spoken to any of the neighbours or the gardener and had no prior knowledge of where she and Bill were going to stay. Despite this, it could never be ruled out that someone had not spoken to her about the former owner of Ardachie.

Peter McEwan's report to the SPR concluded:

Whether Mrs M actually experienced the vision she described and whether her trance-like states were genuine seemed to me matters of minor importance. The important question is surely not the form but the substance of the experiences. Why was it an old lady with a cap on her head and a shawl, why a crawling vision, why feel uneasy in the rose garden, why see a 'wraith' so suddenly on the back stairs and why allude to a rose tree that no one would notice and about its recent history (demise) almost no one knew? The cumulative association with Mrs B is too great to allow an explanation in terms of pure coincidence. We have strong evidence for a neurosis. An additional explanation must, it would seem, be sought in terms of either (a) prior knowledge (which is impossible to exclude conclusively), or (b) some paranormal activity, possibly evoked by the turbulent state of the subconscious mind of Mrs M. The latter hypothesis possesses the least number of inherent contradictions and accounts for the greatest number of facts with most economy.

So Peter McEwan was not wholly against the idea that Frances had indeed picked up on some genuine paranormal activity in the building and had channelled it due to her fraught mental state.

So was Ardachie really haunted? Although it is almost certain that Frances faked some of the phenomena, it does appear that the lodge was the centre of some paranormal activity.

Sometime later a London solicitor and old school friend of Peter McEwan, Bingham Hobson, was staying in the main house. One evening the pair were chatting in the drawing room when they both heard footsteps and the sound of something being dragged across the floor. These sounds appeared to come from the empty room above where they were sitting. Hobson searched the building for an intruder but could find no one. He was quite shaken by this experience and, although a sceptic of the paranormal, decided to return to London.

The Abbot of the nearby Benedictine Abbey also confirmed that a retired local policeman had been doing some jobs at the lodge following Mrs Bruen's death. He had been in the lower kitchen when he heard footsteps outside the door. He opened it just as the footsteps appeared to pass in front of him. He could see no one. He immediately left the property in some panic.

The McEwans decided to sell the estate and eventually moved to Sussex. There was, however, one last curious experience connected with Ardachie and this occurred several years after their departure from the area. Michael Millar, a local dealer in antique firearms, was shooting on a hill above Ardachie when he saw Dorothy McEwan walking along, looking cold and wearing a cardigan. She was accompanied by an old lady. Surprised at seeing her – knowing the McEwans to be now living in England – he called out a greeting but was ignored. Thinking that he had seen her ghost, he contacted Peter McEwan in Sussex and was relieved to hear that Mrs McEwan was alive and well. The mystery of the doppelganger and her elderly companion was never solved. However, it does bring to mind the claim made by Frances McDonald that she had seen the double of Mrs McEwan during her brief stay in the house.

In 1977 the haunting was dramatised by the BBC in their paranormal series Leap in the Dark. Colin Wilson, the noted author and researcher, was the presenter. The producer of the series tracked down the McDonalds and asked them about the haunting. It turned out that Frances was very bitter about the McEwans and stated that they had let her and her husband down as, 'they should have told us the place was haunted before we went.' It should also be noted that during the interview she never admitted to faking any paranormal activity during her time at Ardachie.

No one lived at Ardachie after the McEwans left. In 1968 the main building was blown up by the army after it was condemned as unsafe. The new landowner then had the place levelled with bulldozers. Nothing now remains of the house or its alleged ghost.

Chapter 13

THE AGONY OF MARIE LE MOYNE

B arnwell Castle in Northamptonshire was built in the 13th century by Berengar le Moyne. It is now a ruin but has acquired a sinister reputation due to unexplained occurrences in the neighbourhood of the castle. Once, a policeman patrolling the area encountered a rushing wind on an otherwise windless night. On another occasion, the village postmaster was out walking his dog when the animal suddenly broke free and ran towards the ruined castle. The postmaster chased the dog to the southern side of the ruins, near the gatehouse, when he too was caught up in a gale of wind which seemed to rush past him. The dog, apparently terrified by this, ran home and was found by the postmaster on the doorstep, shaking with fear.

It is also reported that in the 1930s another policeman had experienced similar phenomena in one particular area – the north-east tower – and vowed that he would not return there 'for all the tea in China'.

Tom Litchfield, a local historian, was intrigued by these tales and decided to find out what was behind these strange occurrences. In 1948 Mr Litchfield and an engineer friend of his, who was psychic, carried out a series of seances using a Ouija board in an attempt to contact the spirit or spirits responsible for the haunting at Barnwell Castle.

Three seances were held in total. The first two were carried out at Litchfield's house in Barnwell, the third taking place in the ruined north-east tower of the castle.

The first attempt took place on 20 September 1948 and contact was made with an entity claiming to be a former Abbot of Ramsey Abbey. The Abbot stated that the castle had been used as a court of justice and execution

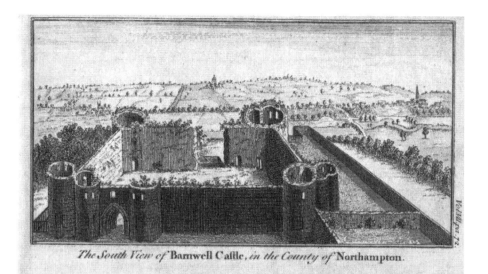

Barnwell Castle. (public domain)

in the 14th century. This information was later found to be correct when Litchfield checked local historical records.

At the mention of executions, the identity of the spirit appeared to change and the messages became more detailed. The spirit claimed to have been 'Marie, uxor (wife) of le Moyne'. It then referred to 'horror and untimely death' and mentioned a chest hidden in a dungeon where the remnants of a 'ruined life' resided – the ruined life being hers. Her death, according to the communication, had taken place while the castle was still being built.

The spirit was then asked, 'How was your life ruined?' The reply was short and to the point, 'By heathen rule enforcing a brutish captivity.' Litchfield and his companion then asked for the identity of her tormentor but she declined with the words, 'Secret. I can never betray my soul's secret.' All she would say was that it was a terrible death and that, 'He came quietly. Play not for time, he will win the race.' The messages then stopped.

Litchfield decided to research the claims made at the seance and found that a local tradition credited one of the Le Moyne lords (Berengar) with walling up a woman alive in the castle. It was also discovered that a woman called Marie – wife of the lord – had indeed died during the castle's construction.

The second seance held on 30 September 1948 proved just as rewarding in terms of information. A Reginald Le Moyne came through but quickly handed over the communication to Berengarius le Moyne, who was described as his successor and also mysteriously as the 'second bastion'.

Berengarius was asked about what lay in the bastion and he replied, 'The horrid remnants of suppression which befell an honest lord. William forced my reason.' The inquirers then asked who was William? 'We call him covert in Ramsey' was the reply. It emerged that William was a contemporary with Berengarius. He was William, Abbot of Godmanchester, and a contemporary of Berengarius. It emerged that Berengarius had sold the castle and lands to the abbey in 1276. It was unknown why Berengarius had sold William the property. Had it been done under duress? The message from Berengarius seemed to imply this. Had William become aware of the fate of Marie le Moyne? Was acquiring the castle the price he demanded for his silence?

The third and final seance was held on 9 November 1948 in the north-east tower of the castle. It was to prove terrifying.

The Ouija board was placed on a stone slab and a storm lantern was lit to illuminate the ruined tower. The seance then began. Berengarius immediately came through and was asked what he wanted to say. 'I will fire to warn you,' was his ominous reply.

Suddenly above and behind the heads of Litchfield and his companion came the crack of a whip or gun. When the two men turned, they saw to their horror the head and upper body of a monk standing in the doorway to the courtyard. It was not surprising that upon seeing the apparition, they fled the tower and raced home.

Tom Litchfield resolved to cease all further attempts at communication with the spirits of Barnwell Castle and became convinced that the use of the Ouija board in the investigation had been a mistake. Despite this, part of him still remained curious about the case. He decided to visit All Saints Church at Sawtrey near Barnwell, where members of the Le Moyne family were commemorated in brass memorial tablets. It was here that he noticed the insignia of the Le Moynes – it was the upper torso of a monk and in the monk's hands was a whip or flail!

So what are we to make of this case? That the evidence given in the seances later proved correct is certainly true. The names given during the first two seances proved historically correct, including the fact that a lady called Marie le Moyne had died during the construction of the castle. This also tied in with local traditions concerning a murder and concealment in the castle walls. And let us not forget the startling appearance of the phantom monk and the subsequent discovery that the emblem of the Le Moynes was indeed a monk. So in this case the use of the Ouija board had proved useful ... or so it appeared.

I have always been wary of Ouija boards and remain very sceptical as to their use in paranormal investigations. Can we be sure that the spirit wishing to speak is the person who it claims to be? And is it really a spirit or something more sinister? I can well recall a medium once telling me to stay clear of Ouija boards. She explained that you could never be sure what may be tempted to come through. She likened it to leaving your front door wide open with the offer 'please enter my home and do as you wish.' I can well remember a lady who once mocked my aunt's use of the Ouija board during one of her regular psychic demonstrations. The glass was seen to levitate and fly towards the lady in question. It missed her by inches, smashing against the wall and sending fragments of glass flying across the room. Is this a power to be taken so lightly? The consequences could certainly prove costly to those who see the Ouija board as simply a toy or a way to impress paying guests or TV viewers during ghost hunts.

Tom Litchfield never forgot what he had witnessed in the ruined tower of Barnwell Castle. He died in 1985, deeply regretting the use of the Ouija board and wishing to his dying day that the horror it had revealed to him could be forever erased from his mind.

So is the skeleton of a murdered woman – Marie le Moyne – really hidden in a secret dungeon in Barnwell Castle? The evidence of the hauntings and the Ouija board sessions do appear to point to the place of concealment as the north-east tower. However, we are unlikely to ever learn the truth as the castle lies on private land and the current owners are content to leave the ruins and any attendant ghosts well alone. But maybe a prayer for the soul of Marie le Moyne and the hope that she can finally find release wouldn't go amiss if you are so inclined to visit the area.

Chapter 14

EALING'S HOUSE OF DEATH

A ndrew Green was one of the most respected paranormal investigators of the 20th century. He lectured on the subject, wrote several books devoted to British hauntings and was greatly in demand by TV documentary makers due to his enthusiasm and knowledge of our ghostly past.

Green's first-ever brush with the supernatural was at the age of 17 and it was an experience which nearly cost him his life!

It was May 1944 and Green's father was a rehousing settlement officer for Ealing Town Council in London. He was looking for a suitable property in which to store furniture from bombed out buildings, and it was hoped that an empty house at 16 Montpelier Road (formally known as Mount Park Road) would be ideal for this purpose. An inspection proved this to be the case, with Green's father confirming that the house 'was highly suitable and free from rising damp, wood rot and furniture beetle.' The only problem that he encountered was the smell of sulphur or gas which appeared mysteriously every 28 days in one of the upstairs rooms. As the smell was not constant, he advised that this part of the house should remain locked and unused.

Workmen were authorised to bring furniture to the house but soon complained of an 'atmosphere' there. They were also concerned to hear footsteps in an upstairs corridor and the sudden disappearance of their tools resulted in them leaving the house after just three hours. They all refused to return, declaring that the house was haunted.

Green was forced to bring in workmen from further afield as the house's sinister reputation had spread. He decided to speak to the local police and discovered from a Sgt. Smith that the Victorian house – originally known as Ellerslie Towers and later renamed Hillcrest Towers – had been the scene of several suicides since its construction in 1883 by Robert Henry Wallace Dunlop, a former colonial judge. In 1887 a 12-year-old girl, Anne Hinchfield, had jumped from a tower and this had been followed by 19 more suicides and a murder, all of which had occurred from the top of the same tower which formed part of the neo-Gothic building.

In September, Green's father was required to inspect the house and asked his son if he would like to visit what he described as a 'haunted house.' Andrew, although not interested in ghosts at the time, was intrigued and readily agreed.

The day for the visit came and Andrew took along his camera to record his exploration of the house. He had a plan of the building and proceeded to inspect the cellar, ground floor and then the upstairs rooms. He soon discovered the 'sulphur room' and, by looking through the keyhole, found that it had once been used as a laboratory – a Bunsen burner and several other items of equipment could still be seen inside.

Green then went up a spiral staircase where he found himself in a circular tower room. He noticed a ladder which led to a trapdoor in the ceiling and, upon climbing it, had the sensation of being physically helped by a pair of hands on his waist. Looking back, he was surprised to see no one. On reaching the top of the tower, he gazed out over the rooftops and then looked down some 70 feet to the crazy paving in the overgrown garden below. It was at this point that he suddenly had the urge to step off the parapet, an inner voice telling him to 'Have a look in the garden. Walk over the parapet, it's only 12 inches on to the lawn. You won't hurt yourself.'

Green sat on the parapet and was about to jump when his father suddenly appeared, grabbing him with the words, 'We don't want any suicides in the family.'

Green later said that at the time he was convinced he would not have been hurt if he had stepped off the parapet and could only wonder if the other suicides had been influenced to jump in the same way. He also noted that the crazy paving below gave the impression of a lack of height and even considered the possibility that black magic had somehow played a part in the deaths as strange magical symbols could be seen carved into the tower's stonework.

It was now 2.30 in the afternoon and Andrew noted a distinct 'atmosphere of malevolence' as he left the now locked and empty house with his father. He decided to take a final picture of the building from the grounds and when the photo was developed the chemist asked him about the young girl looking out from an upstairs window. Green had the photo enlarged and could clearly see the figure of a girl looking out towards him. He wondered if it could have been a trick of the light and the following year he attempted to recreate the photo with a friend from the Royal Photographic Society. Despite taking the photo from the same spot, they failed to duplicate the original figure and later tests by photographic experts and the Society of Psychical Research confirmed that the image on the original photo had not been caused by a double exposure or a fault on the film.

Andrew, like his father before him, visited the local police station and was told of the house's history of suicides, including that of Anne Hinchfield in 1887. Could the 'girl' in the photo have been her?

It was after his first visit that Green was told by his mother, a former nurse, of her involvement with the house in 1934. She and a doctor had been called there after a nursemaid had thrown a young child and then herself from the tower. Green's mother had left the doctor examining the bodies and had walked into the back garden where she suddenly saw footprints appear in the grass. The footsteps were seen to approach a garden seat which moved and rocked as if someone had sat down on it. She later told Dr Pye, the physician, about her strange and upsetting experience. His only reply was that 'Nothing surprises me about that house' but refused to elaborate when she pressed him for more information.

The years went by and the 1950s saw the house converted into several flats. Green had hoped to investigate the property again but the new owner made it quite clear that any talk of ghosts would result in swift legal action after Andrew had made an appeal in a local newspaper requesting further information about the house. It was 1952 and Green was by now a member of a local amateur dramatic society. He discovered that the rehearsals for a play, *The Poltergiest*, were to be held in the very house that he had visited some eight years before! The director of the play was Ken Yandell, a BBC producer. He had no knowledge of the house's reputation but told Green of his belief that the place was haunted, explaining that his dog went 'berserk' every 28 days, snarling and acting as if fighting with an unseen presence on the window. He also complained of a 'foul smell in his bathroom' which occurred every four or five weeks and spoke of hearing strange footsteps within the flat. It turned out that his bathroom was the site of the laboratory seen by Green in 1944.

During their first rehearsal, one of the actors, a Mrs Pyatt, suddenly went into a trance and started to talk like a girl to her shocked colleagues. She said that her name was Anne and explained that she had not killed herself, 'I only wanted to go into the garden, but the roof was higher than I thought.' It should be noted at this point that Green had not told those present of the house's history or its reputation for being haunted.

A week later the second rehearsal was disrupted by the sounds of footsteps walking across the room and the opening and closing of a door. Interestingly, only five of the seven people present heard these sounds.

Problems plagued the production and lack of finances, the death of the male lead in a car crash and another cast member being hurt in a plane crash caused the play to be cancelled.

Two years later Yandell saw Green and told him of a recent brush with death in the house. A party in his flat and several overnight guests had seen him forced to sleep in the bathroom. At 2am his wife had been woken by the sounds of him moaning and gasping for breath in the bath. He was rushed to hospital and the matron there was puzzled as he showed all the signs of sulphur poisoning. She was at a loss to explain how this could have happened as the flat was without gas. She went on to explain that without treatment he would have died within 30 minutes.

Yandell told Green that he had been forced to have his dog put down due to recurrent monthly fits. He also mentioned that other flat owners had experienced strange things in the house. One couple had heard the sounds of a 'limping man with a walking stick' walking through their living room and bedroom. It emerged that their flat incorporated the corridor which had led to the suicide tower. Another couple, who lived in the tower itself, had witnessed their front door bell being pushed by an unseen person as they sat relaxing in the garden.

In 1960 Green was a guest on a TV show called *Jim's Inn* starring Jimmy Hanley. Jack Edwardes, one of the script writers, spoke of some trouble he was having with a recurrent monthly smell of sulphurous gas in his bathroom. He went on to say that the Gas Board had failed to find the cause as there were no gas pipes in the house. He had also been bothered by the sound of footsteps. He lived at 16 Montpelier Road.

The house was pulled down in 1970 and replaced by a block of flats, known as Elgin Court, which was built slightly to the south of the old building. Green discovered that the residents there spoke of hearing unusual banging noises but was unable to discover more.

In 1973 Andrew wrote about the house in his book, *Our Haunted Kingdom*, and began to receive letters from people who were familiar with or had lived in the house. One spoke of the house's reputation for suicides dating back to at least 1912, while another, Mrs Laycock, wrote of her time there as a young maid in 1922. This was during the residence of a Mrs Nellie Theresa Demery. She recalled a butler named Tanner who had once worked for the royal household in Kensington Palace. The butler had been injured in a coach accident during his time at the palace and had been left with a limp. One day Mrs Laycock said she had been sorting out boxes in the lumber-room when she noticed a loose floorboard. Underneath it was a case baring a royal crest and the words *Kensington Palace*. Inside were four cut-throat razors with gold and tortoiseshell handles. These were wrapped in newspaper articles which mentioned both the Jack the Ripper murders and the Duke of Clarence, Queen Victoria's grandson. She also told Green of her belief that the female owners of the house were involved in witchcraft as every Friday the tower room, now painted black, was used for a ritual using black candles. None of the servants were allowed in the room except for the butler, who would give her the used candlesticks for cleaning. The maid left the house in April and later learned that the butler had killed himself by taking laudanum. The suicide had been hushed up by the owners of the house who claimed that his death had been accidental.

Green was inclined to dismiss Mrs Laycock's claims as fantasy, influenced by a now largely discredited theory that the Duke of Clarence had been the notorious Jack the Ripper. He was also unable to obtain further clarification of the suicides and murder at 16 Montpelier Road as police records for the years in question had been destroyed.

Green never forgot his strange experiences in Ealing and often returned to the subject in lectures and in his books. He died in 2004 and his archive was taken over by the author and lawyer Alan Murdie. By chance, he found himself dealing with the will of a deceased lady who had been the partner of Ian Wallace Dunlop, a member of the first family to own 16 Montpelier Road.

Ian, a man in his 80s, was dismissive of the large number of suicides credited to the house but did recall hearing of a female servant who may have killed herself there in the 19th century. He could not recall the name Anne Hinchfield, the alleged first suicide, and said that the family had vacated the house around the year 1916 for financial reasons and not because of any ghosts or scandals connected with the property. Of the later residents and the talk of Jack the Ripper, black magic and murder, he could offer nothing apart from the comment that rumours of black magic rituals being held in the house were 'ridiculous.'

So was the late Ian Wallace Dunlop right in dismissing the house's sinister reputation as nothing more than rumour and tall tales? As much as I respect his opinion, I cannot agree with him. For instance, it must be noted that Wallace Dunlop had no direct experience of what had occurred in the house as he had not even been born when his family vacated 16 Montpelier Road. His dismissal of black magic rituals being held there is also worthless as these are alleged to have occurred in the years after his family had ceased to have any connection with the property.

One or two claims of paranormal activity would be easy to ignore but we have too many witnesses and evidence to dismiss the haunting of 16 Montpelier Road as mere fantasy. The phenomena witnessed and felt by Green and others clearly shows that something strange and sinister was connected to the building, a force that was both malevolent and a physical danger to all those who came within its influence.

Travel to 16 Montpelier Road today and you will find Elgin Court standing isolated and somewhat forlorn in a road largely lined by Victorian and Edwardian houses and flats. Residents in the block still occasionally complain of strange knocks and other sounds within the flats. Others have also described a feeling of 'heaviness' when visiting the site of the original house – slightly to the north of Elgin Court – and have expressed a sense of relief upon leaving the area. The site of the suicide tower is now empty air and one can only hope that it will always remain so.

Chapter 15

THE LADY AND THE BUTTERFLY

The Theatre Royal in Bath dates back to 1805 and has been described by the Theatres Trust as 'one of the most important surviving examples of Georgian theatre architecture.' It has also been hailed as the most haunted theatre in Britain and can boast several ghosts. One of the most frequently seen is that of the Grey Lady. There is no record of her name but legend claims that she was an actress who attracted the attentions of a man who used to come night after night to watch her perform, his favourite box being the one where her spirit was later seen to appear. Her husband is supposed to have found out about his potential rival and killed the man in a duel. Upon discovering this, his distraught wife committed suicide by throwing herself from a theatre window.

Another variation of the story claims that she hanged herself in the Garrick's Head pub which lies next to the theatre. And to make matters even more confusing, in this version it is stated that she was not an actress but a patron of the theatre in love with one of the actors there!

Theatre Royal, Bath. (public domain)

All that can be said with any certainty is that many people in the theatre over the years have reported seeing a ghostly woman wearing a long grey dress, sometimes with feathers in her hair. Her favourite spot is the top left-hand box above the stage but she has also been seen in other parts of the theatre including the stalls, corridors, stage and upper circle. She often appears solid but at other times has appeared almost smoke-like in appearance. She has also occasionally been seen in the Garrick's Head.

In 1920 the Russian ballerina, Anna Pavlova, was performing at the theatre and asked about the solitary lady in feathers in an old-fashioned grey dress whom she saw sitting in a box near the stage. She was surprised to learn that the box in question had been unoccupied during her performance. In 1975 Dame Anna Neagle also had an encounter during a performance of *The Dame of Sark*. She saw a smoke-like pillar appear on stage which slowly turned into a woman in old-fashioned looking clothes. The figure then slowly drifted off stage into the wings. Audience members also saw it, several of whom scrambled over seats in order to escape the theatre. Two Canadian ladies said that they first saw the apparition appear in the haunted box. She appeared in a hazy greenish mist and then suddenly dissolved into 'spinning smoke' before reappearing on the stage next to the actress. Dame Anna was so shocked by the encounter that she refused to work in the theatre again.

On another occasion, a child was seen by her father speaking to someone in the haunted box. He could see no one but the child later described seeing and talking to 'a pretty lady who smelt nice.' She also said she was 'all puddly', which the father later learned was his daughter's word for smoke.

One staff member left her job after seeing a figure in a grey dress and grey shoes standing near her. She had first noticed her after bending down to pick up some keys, which she had dropped. The figure made a sigh and a swishing sound as it started to move. The terrified woman fled in terror. Others have described the figure as being accompanied by a scent of jasmine and have gone on to say that they felt strangely depressed after seeing her.

One lady in the 1960s saw her in the lighting box during a performance. She was manning a spotlight when she heard the door open and someone enter the box behind her. She saw nothing but then became aware of an icy chill and the smell of perfume. She then noticed a woman in a hood crouching in the corner. Her clothes gave off a silvery sheen and she appeared to be nodding or rocking. She then slowly faded away. Not surprisingly, the lady fled the scene only to become aware of the lighting box door being flung open violently behind her and cold wind rushing past her down the stairs. After that experience she refused to work in the lighting box unless accompanied by another member of staff.

A front of house staff member had a very strange experience which may or may not be connected to the Grey Lady. He had been taking crates to the Upper Circle Bar when he heard what sounded like a long sigh and muffled moaning from the auditorium. He opened the doors to see what was making the noise and saw three shapes which looked like stooped figures. Two of these were semi-transparent while the third leading figure was grey in colour and appeared to be more solid. All three were drifting through the seats. It appeared that the grey figure was sighing while the other two were moaning. The three figures then appeared to realise that they were being watched and stopped, turning as if to face him. The sound then changed to what sounded like birds singing and all three apparitions suddenly merged into a black rectangle which appeared to be about two-foot long. This then changed into a triangle and flew up towards a chandelier at great speed where it promptly vanished. It comes as no surprise that he resigned his job and left never to return.

Objects disappearing and then reappearing, footsteps in deserted areas of the theatre and doors opening of their own accord are also attributed to the Grey Lady. Sightings of the apparition continue to the present day.

However, the Grey Lady is not alone in the theatre. She must share centre stage with a strange fluttering butterfly that has been seen as both an omen of misfortune and success!

In 1948 the theatre was being run by the Maddox family, the senior member being Reg Maddox, the theatre's manager and producer. He had decided that the Christmas production that year should be *Little Red Riding Hood*. The show featured girls dressed as butterflies and also included a butterfly backdrop as part of the set design. During rehearsals a dead tortoiseshell butterfly was found on the stage. The coincidence of the butterfly theme of the show was remarked upon but little was thought of this until a few hours later when Reg Maddox collapsed and died of a heart attack as he was lighting a scene.

Theatre folk are generally regarded as being very superstitious and it comes as little surprise to learn that some in the cast and production crew regarded the sudden appearance of the dead butterfly as an omen of Reg's death.

Frank Maddox, Reg's son, took over the production of the pantomime and it was decided to remove the butterfly theme. However, this decision was soon reversed after another tortoiseshell butterfly suddenly appeared very much alive fluttering above the stage.

Frank decided that this was more than a coincidence and felt that this new butterfly's appearance was a good omen. His reasons for thinking this are not clear but he may have been influenced by a folk tradition which claims that a living butterfly represents the soul of someone who has died. Whatever the reason, he reinstated the butterfly ballet, becoming firmly convinced that the butterfly was connected to the spirit of his father and that its appearance would guarantee a successful pantomime season. His hunch proved right.

Since then, the butterfly has appeared several times and its sudden appearance has always coincided with a money-making production.

In December 1979 the late Leslie Crowther was playing Wishy-Washy in *Aladdin* at the theatre. He was aware of the butterfly tradition and had noted that it had so far failed to appear:

> *I must say that nothing was further from my mind when I prepared in the wings to make my entrance in the Boxing Day matinee, but then a miracle happened. After Reg Maddox had allowed me sufficient time to establish a rapport with the audience he fluttered down from the spotlight in the form of a tortoiseshell butterfly and alighted on my left shoulder! I gently scooped it/him up and then released it/him into the wings, meanwhile telling the audience that I would tell them at the end of the performance why I was looking so gob-smacked – which I did.*
>
> *Dear old Reg – he stuck around for days and days. Sometimes we spotted him in the front of the house and sometimes back-stage, but I'll never forget the first time he fluttered down from the spotlight. And yes! The pantomime was a big success.*

In 1982 the theatre reopened after a refurbishment. A gala performance of *A Midsummer's Night Dream* was held, with Princess Margaret in attendance. The actors and audience, including the Princess, all saw a butterfly flying above the stage in a clockwise direction throughout the play.

In 1985 the actress Honor Blackman also witnessed the lucky butterfly. She was doing a press call at the theatre when a butterfly appeared from nowhere. Needless to say the pantomime, *Jack and the Beanstalk*, was a great success!

On another occasion a butterfly was seen tapping against a window on the very day that the box office reached £100,000 in takings.

Peter O'Toole also had an encounter with the butterfly during a run of *Jeffrey Bernard is Unwell*. The production had been troubled and it was speculated that it would be cancelled as the audience's reaction to the play was less than encouraging. During a matinee performance the actor was in the middle of a scene when a tortoiseshell butterfly was seen to walk on stage towards him. The butterfly then took flight and flew three times round the actor's head before landing on his newspaper. It then took flight again, circling Peter's head another three times before flying off towards the ceiling. The actor ad libbed about the butterfly's unscheduled part in the play and carried on with his performance. One of the crew above the stage made a grab for the butterfly but found that he had grabbed thin air. Following the appearance of the butterfly, things began to improve for the play, with Peter O'Toole eventually taking it to the West End where it received rave reviews and sell-out houses.

The butterfly was also seen in the 2010 Christmas season during another run of *Aladdin*. Cast members, production staff and the audience all saw a butterfly flutter across the stage and into the stalls. The show proved another triumph.

The original butterfly backdrop scenery from the 1948 production has also been preserved as another symbol of good luck for the theatre and now hangs in the fly tower. In 1981 it was temporally removed during renovations. During its absence several members of the stage crew decided to sort through a store cupboard full of old theatre props. They came across a wooden box and upon opening it inadvertently released six tortoiseshell butterflies which proceeded to fly off in the direction of the main theatre building. No one was sure how the butterflies had got in there as the box had clearly been locked and sealed for years. Upon closer inspection of the box, a dusty and faded photo bearing the year 1932 was discovered. The photo was of Reg Maddox!

Chapter 16

BEYOND HARRY PRICE – THE GHOSTS OF BORLEY CHURCH

Borley Rectory was once said to be the most haunted house in England. Harry Price's investigation of the case still creates controversy to this day, with his defenders and critics equally convinced that Price was either the foremost paranormal investigator of his day or a fame-hungry charlatan.

Price's interest in the rectory appears to have diverted his attention from the medieval church which, judging from the evidence, is just as badly haunted as the rectory once was. Price was aware of activity being reported in the church and was told by Ethel Bull (a member of the original family at the rectory) that coffins in the Waldegrave family vault underneath the building had been found to have mysteriously moved when the vault was opened up in the 19th century. Sadly, he did little to follow up such leads.

The Reverend Harry Bull, rector of Borley from 1892 until his death in 1927, was the first known person to experience unusual activity in the church. He was inside with a friend when they both heard tapping outside. The sounds grew louder and actually appeared to enter the building. The taps then moved around the church, with Bull and his companion following them. The pair examined the church and churchyard but found nothing to account for the sounds.

Another rector, the Reverend Alfred Henning, rector of Borley and Liston from 1936 to 1955, readily admitted that strange things occurred there and even published a short book devoted to the ghosts of Borley.

On 24 April 1949 Henning went to Borley to hold evensong. He was surprised to find the church door locked and went to Mrs Pearson, the lady in charge of the keys, to ask why she had not unlocked it. It turned out that

Previously unpublished signed photograph of Harry Price. (Stewart Evans)

she had missed his announcement of the service in the parish magazine but had assumed the rector had been in the church earlier that day as she and her husband had both distinctly heard the church bells ringing at 8am. At the time, and unbeknown to her, the building had been securely locked.

Henning also mentions another incident in 1946 when several children in the church were there to attend a Sunday catechism class. As they were early, they sat by the organ, waiting for their teacher, Miss Byford, to arrive. All the children heard footsteps coming up the church path and the sound of someone locking the church door. One of the children, Kathleen Finch, went to the door and called out but received no response. The children naturally became frightened as they could not get out. A few minutes passed and Miss Byford arrived and found that the door was still locked. Fortunately, she was able to release the children.

The church path appears to be one of the main centres of activity with a large number of people reporting hearing the sounds of footsteps on the gravel. On 21 April 1946 John Durrant, from Sudbury, and his fiancée were looking round the church. They were both inside when they heard footsteps in the porch and the noise of the latch being lifted. The door failed to open and Mr Durrant opened it to see who was there. He was surprised to find the porch and churchyard empty.

In 1947 Harry Price was invited by Henning to look at the restored altar in the church – Price had helped pay for its restoration:

We took him up to Borley at half past five in the evening. No one was about and we went up to the chancel, leaving the west door open. While we stood there talking about the altar, we were interrupted by an insistent and prolonged screeching of birds near the west end. I should almost describe it as a panic screaming of the rooks, which inhabit the elms overhanging the tower. I have often heard the birds make the usual noise when coming on and off their nests, but nothing approaching the din which was now going on behind us. Mr. Price asked, 'Do they always go on like that?' and I had to say that, as far as I knew, the

Borley Church. (John West)

noise was unusual. I think what I really meant was that I had grown so used to the birds and the noise they made that generally I did not notice them. The very fact that I was now noticing them pointed to the noise being out of the ordinary. But the noise died down and, in the stillness after the birds were at rest again, came the sound of footsteps in the porch. I thought to myself, 'What a pity. Visitors are coming in just when we wanted to be undisturbed to talk.' We waited for people to appear but no one came. I hurried down the church thinking someone had heard our voices and did not like to enter. I was astonished to find no one in the porch and, going quickly through the churchyard, I looked up and down the road. There was not a soul to be seen.

Henning also reported that footsteps and the sounds of terrified birds were again heard by him the following Saturday. Two visiting student friends were witnesses to this.

In September 1947 John May of Bury St Edmunds travelled to Borley from Bury to look around the village and churchyard. He arrived there at 10.30pm. It was a warm and windless night and the only sounds were coming from cattle and owls. He started to drift off to sleep in the porch when the noise of the church gate opening and the sounds of footsteps coming up the path woke him up:

> *The light was clear. The footsteps continued but there was no one near. I*
> *sensed someone passing me, there was a chilliness in the air and I felt a*
> *slight pressure. Whatever it was, I knew and felt that it was essentially*
> *evil. I also knew that I resented in some way hearing and not seeing.*
> *I then heard the sound of a key in the lock, then the creak of the door*
> *hinges as the door opened. I heard the door close. A few seconds later*
> *I heard soft notes and chords from the organ. The time was 12.18am.*

The church was still locked on examination. May described the music as tuneless. He stayed until 2.30am but nothing further occurred.

Reverend Henning also heard the sound of music coming from the building. On one occasion, he was visiting the church with the novelist Norah Burke. It was October 1947. The time was 3.15pm:

> *As we were walking up the path to the south door (the path on which the*
> *footsteps have been heard) I stopped and said, 'The organ is playing.'*
> *My first thought was that there was a service in progress and that we*
> *could not therefore go in. The rector stopped and looked at me. He*
> *heard it too; he of course knew that there was no service going on.*

A search of the church revealed it to be empty and the organ securely locked. The novelist described the brief 30 seconds snatch of music as being like the sort played 'while the collection is being taken or waiting for a bride.'

Some locals did suggest that air left in the bellows was responsible for the mysterious music. To test this theory, Henning pumped up the organ and left it. The air escaped immediately and pressing the keys produced no sound. It was then claimed that two local boys had sneaked into the church to play the organ and then hide when anyone approached. This is a possibility but it would not explain the music heard when the church and organ were both locked.

Stuart Kiernander, a paranormal investigator, visited the church in 1947 and saw what he described as a 'mysterious figure or white shape' pass the porch as he was reading. Two years later he revisited the area and held vigil in the church porch. He heard footsteps along the path but could see nothing. He resumed his seat and about 30 minutes later he again heard the sound of someone walking up the path. They approached the porch and Kiernander rushed out to see who was there. The path was empty.

Kiernander again returned to Borley two years later and found himself once again sitting in the brick porch. The footsteps were absent this time but the sounds of taps and clicks could clearly be heard coming from the church door.

The poet and author, James Turner, also heard the sound of 'something or somebody with a lame leg and a swishing skirt' walking along the church path.

I have also had two strange experiences on the path, but more of that later!

The smell of incense has been noticed along the path and inside the church. Others have claimed to have smelt decaying flesh. One witness to this, Susanna Dudley, was visiting Borley one February day with three friends, Miss Audrey Sawrey-Cookson, Sub-Lt. Alastair MacIver RN and Sub-Lt. Jonathan Crossley RN:

> *I can't describe the smell really, as I have never smelt anything like it before in my life ... Personally, the thought that passed my mind was that it smelt as I imagine balm – an embalmed body, would smell! I have no foundation for this, as I have never smelt an embalmed body. But at the time, a sudden thought of 'disgusting, like an embalmed body' struck me, so if you can imagine, too, an embalmed body – that sickly*

sweet clinging smell, heavy and nasty – that's just what it was like ... I
think the fact it was February disproved any idea of 'flowering bushes'
or fertiliser – and it wasn't pig as since suggested by one of the papers.

She also said that the smell was confined to an area roughly three yards long that you could walk in and out of. A strong wind was blowing at the time and yet the smell was still in the same spot when the group returned ten minutes later. Sawrey-Cookson thought that the smell resembled incense while MacIver described the smell as 'the most disgusting thing he had ever smelt'. It is interesting to note that Crossley was unable to notice the odour despite having an excellent sense of smell.

In the 1970s a couple, Mr and Mrs Clinton, smelt incense in two separate spots in the churchyard. This was also despite a strong wind blowing at the time.

The famous Borley nun (whose supposed partial remains were found in the rectory cellars) has been seen in the churchyard on several occasions.

In August 1949 the Reverend Stanley C. Kipling was at Borley to read the lesson at a friend's funeral. He had changed into his gown and was near the porch when he spotted a veiled woman in the churchyard. She walked behind a yew tree, reappeared and then vanished. He went over to the spot where she had disappeared but could find nothing. He described her as being roughly 18 to 23 years of age, looked frail and was wearing a nun's hood. Kipling had been very sceptical of the Borley ghosts and Price's claims until this incident.

In October 1949 two men were visiting Borley at night. They were in the porch when they heard sounds from inside the church. At 11.48pm a figure in black was seen in the churchyard walking towards the priest's door where it vanished.

A former resident of the rectory cottage, Terence Bacon, also saw her on three occasions. She appeared to be gliding some two feet above the churchyard ground.

In July 1952 Mr Cole of Great Cornard, who used to cut the grass in the churchyard, saw the figure of a nun standing between a gap in the hedge on

Borley Church. (John West)

the north side of the church. She appeared to be about five feet six inches tall. She was solid and wore a black hood, gold-coloured bodice, white collar and a black skirt which was open, revealing a blue under-garment. It was a windy day and he thought she may be waiting for someone. He approached her to ask if she wanted to wait in the church porch and, as he did so, she vanished.

On 20 June 1970 a shrouded figure was seen walking down the church path by Mr R. G. Croom-Hollingsworth, a paranormal investigator. He radioed to his two colleagues, Mr F. Connell and Mr R. Potter, who rushed to join him. The figure had disappeared behind a yew tree and a search revealed nothing. Soon after this, the group saw a light from inside the church. It appeared to move towards the altar. A check of the church door confirmed that it was locked.

An hour and a half later, Croom-Hollingsworth saw the figure again. This time, it was on the site of the old rectory. It was gliding a foot above the ground and actually came within 15 feet of him. He described her as appearing sad with 'hard and dry' skin. She appeared to be about 60. She had a mole on her left cheek and her eyes were closed. Her clothing was grey and something resembling a shawl covered her head. Potter witnessed her too, standing opposite his colleague. As he approached, the figure turned and walked through a fence and disappeared; it had been visible for some 12 minutes.

In 1974 Croom-Hollingsworth and his colleagues were allowed to hold vigils in the church. The building was searched before each vigil and then the building was sealed to prevent anyone entering. They were joined in the investigation by Denny Densham, a BBC film director.

Tape recorders were left running and these produced the sounds of raps, bumps, bangs, a latch being lifted and a door being opened, human sighs, something being thrown to the ground, footsteps and a sinister grunt. Members of the team also saw a glow of light near the door and pinpricks of light on the curtains near the font and on the pews. Densham called the experience 'quite baffling'. The recordings later formed part of a BBC television documentary featuring Densham and Peter Underwood. Clips from this, including the audio recordings, are available on YouTube.

The church interior has witnessed other strange phenomena. Mrs Bull, a member of the original family to live in the rectory, revisited the church in 1947. She offered to arrange flowers for Easter Sunday and spent most of the proceeding Saturday working on a suitable display. When she had finished the church was locked. On Sunday morning it was found that the flowers had been strewn across the interior. It was thought that vandals may have found their way into the building but a search could find no trace of a forced entry. Harry Price was informed by Henning that a sanctuary lamp wick was constantly being removed each morning despite the church having being locked overnight. He asked the lady in charge of the lamp, Mrs Pearson, to place a book over the lamp glass to prevent it happening again. The next day, the book was found thrown to the ground with such force that the cover had been ripped away. Further attempts to cover the lamp resulted in the covers being thrown to the floor.

The Reverend Henning also mentions a water bottle and man's cap being moved in the porch despite it being empty at the time. On another occasion, a mat in the church was found to have moved.

Henning, in his booklet on Borley, tells of a lady from Sudbury who felt a presence in the porch and then found herself being followed up the aisle of the church by limping footsteps. She naturally became very frightened and made to leave the church. She was shocked to find the footsteps following her, only ceasing as she crossed the porch. Henning pointed out that she was wearing rubber soled shoes at the time and so echoes from her own footsteps could be ruled out as an explanation.

Charles Chilton MBE, a BBC Executive, was visiting the church with a friend. They went inside and suddenly heard the sounds of a violent storm raging outside. Upon leaving the building, they were surprised to find that all was still calm.

Some investigators believe that the Waldgrave monument is the centre of paranormal activity in the church. The Waldgraves were Lords of the Manor of Borley for some 300 years and some investigators believe that the Borley nun is connected to them as they were a prominent Catholic family of the area.

The Reverend Henning reported three loud knocks coming from the area of the memorial during a confirmation class. Michael Bentine, the famed comedian and psychic, once visited the church with a BBC TV crew and felt a zone of coldness around the monument. In 1977 the writer Marc Alexander visited the church with Cheryl Carter, a psychic. She became very stressed and had to leave as she felt that 'negative forces were coming from the tomb.' Alexander felt nothing but decided to return to his car for two copper dowsing rods. He then re-entered the church and walked towards the memorial, the rods held lightly in each hand. Both rods reacted violently when they came within four feet of the monument. By walking back and forth, he confirmed that an invisible square of energy surrounded the area of the memorial. He later told the famed author Colin Wilson of this. Wilson became convinced that the church stood on the intersection of two ley lines and felt that the junction of lines was acting as a catalyst for the psychic activity in the vicinity.

Photos taken in the churchyard have sometimes revealed odd images. The late Sir Simon Marsden took a photograph that showed a strange black shape hanging in mid-air and a nun-like figure was captured on camera by Eddie Brazil in 1972.

I have visited Borley Church on five occasions. The first two visits proved uneventful but on my third visit I was walking up the church path when I suddenly entered what I can only describe as a three foot square zone of intense fear. This feeling lasted just a few seconds. I also visited the church in November 2017 to appear in a short film drama playing a writer investigating the ghosts of Borley. I was standing alone on the church path between takes when my mobile phone proceeded to take 49 photos in rapid succession. Each frame, on inspection, was completely blank. The phone then suddenly switched to video and recorded a few seconds of what sounds like someone walking down the gravel path. I was standing still at the time! I should add that my hand was nowhere near the phone when this occurred. I am at a loss to explain this bizarre behaviour as I have never had any problems with the phone before or since.

It seems that the legend of Borley is still very much in the making!

Chapter 17

THE CURSE OF THE SETONS

The belief that the ancient Egyptians placed curses on all those who defiled their tombs is now firmly established in popular culture largely thanks to horror films and stories from the likes of Bram Stoker, Conan Doyle and Anne Rice. As a child, I can well remember being both horrified and thrilled as I sat in front of the TV and watched Boris Karloff or Christopher Lee emerge from the tomb to seek vengeance on all those who had disturbed their eternal rest. It was only as I grew up that I discovered such tales were largely inspired by the belief that the opening of the tomb of Tutankhamun had resulted in many of those involved dying in mysterious or tragic circumstances due to a curse placed upon the tomb by the priests of the old gods. I then became aware of other incidents involving alleged Egyptian curses, some of which were as terrifying as any offering from the film studios of Universal or Hammer …

Sir Alexander Hay Seton, born in 1904, was the 10th Baronet of Abercorn and Armour Bearer to the Queen. His family could trace their Scottish origins back centuries but by the early 20th century much of their power and wealth had gone. In 1936 Seton and Zeyla, his wife of nine years, were in Egypt on a sightseeing tour. It was during their stay in Cairo that Abdul, a hotel worker, informed them of the

Sir Alexander Hay Seton. (public domain)

157

discovery of a small tomb near the world famous pyramids at Giza. For a fee, the man's brother would take them there. Seton was not particularly interested and later wrote of 'a feeling in my bones that something was going to happen over this and it was only with the greatest of difficulty that Zeyla cajoled me into going with her. I wish earnestly to God that we had not gone!'

Zeyla Seton in 1928.

After breakfast, the couple left with the guide and made their way to the tomb which Seton believed dated back some four or five thousand years. It contained the remains of an unnamed but obviously wealthy woman. The tomb had once been flooded by the Nile and as they arrived workers were still clearing away the ancient solidified mud.

As Seton later recalled in his unpublished memoirs, 'We went down some roughly hewn rock steps – about 30 of them – and there, lying on a stone slab and uncovered was the remains of a skeleton – water and mud had removed most. You could see the skull quite clearly and the leg bones but few ribs were left, although the spine was almost intact.'

Seton pondered on his own mortality as he gazed at the crumbling bones and muttered a short prayer. Eventually, the couple returned to the surface where Seton smoked a cigarette. Zeyla decided to return to the tomb for one more look before the couple returned to the Mena Hotel.

That same evening, Zeyla told her husband that she had taken a bone from the skeleton as a souvenir. 'She showed it to me and to my eyes it looked like a digestive biscuit apart from it being slightly convex and the shape of a heart.' The bone was a sacrum, a triangular bone found at the base of the spine. Seton thought little of it and the object was soon packed along with their other mementoes in readiness for their return journey to their home at 15 Learmonth Gardens in Edinburgh.

Back in Scotland, the couple decided to hold an evening dinner party for their friends. The talk soon turned to their trip to Egypt and the bone was shown to their guests. It excited little comment and Sir Alexander decided to leave the relic in an old carriage clock case on the dining table as the party left for the drawing room. An hour passed and the guests decided to leave. As they made their way down the pathway that led from the front door, a piece of stone from the roof parapet broke free and crashed into the garden below. It only just missed them.

The bone and the display case were moved to the drawing room. The following week, their young daughter's live-in-nanny, Miss Janet Clarke, came to the couple's bedroom in some agitation after hearing what she thought was a burglar in the drawing room. Sir Alexander made his way downstairs to confront the intruder. A search proved fruitless but the following morning it was found that the corner table, on which the bone was kept, had been knocked over. The display case and the bone were scattered on the floor. Seton then recalled a dream from the previous night in which he had heard a noise from downstairs. He assumed that the vibration from passing traffic had caused the table to fall over. Zeyla, on the other hand, thought Seton had knocked it over during his search of the house the night before.

From this moment on, the Setons were disturbed by noises in the house. On one occasion, they heard someone walking on the stairs. Assuming it was the nanny, the couple were at first unconcerned but a search revealed only an empty stairway. It emerged that the nanny had still not returned from an evening out. A few days passed and Alasdair Black, a nephew of the couple, came to stay and was housed in the spare bedroom. One night, as he left a downstairs toilet, he claimed to have seen a figure dressed in strange-looking garments ascending the stairs. Seton became convinced that someone was entering the house in order to steal valuables and decided to hold a vigil in order to catch the would-be thief.

The following night, Sir Alexander readied himself on the upstairs landing after making sure that the windows and drawing room door were securely fastened and the rest of the household were all in bed.

For hours I watched from the balcony outside our bedroom, feeling rather foolish doing so. Nothing happened so I went to bed, only to be rudely awakened by a yell from Zeyla that someone was downstairs. Grabbing my revolver, I dashed downstairs to be met by a very scared nanny. Of course the door was locked and the key still in my pocket. I yelled to Zeyla to get the key and when we finally got in it looked as if a battle royal had taken place there. Chairs were upset, books flung about, and there in the middle of the chaos was that damn Bone, looking as harmless and more like a biscuit than ever.

A check of the windows showed them to be still locked and it was determined that access down the chimney was impossible. Sir Alexander concluded that a poltergeist was responsible with the activity centred on the bone. His wife consulted a 'soothsayer' who offered nothing in the way of support but still demanded a £1 for her services.

The weeks that followed continued to see the Seton household plagued by noises and by furniture being moved. Moving the bone to another location in the house made no difference, 'As usual there it was – *the Bone* – on the floor, and as much furniture as could be was tipped up all over the place.'

The bone was returned to the drawing room. The trouble continued as Seton later recorded in his unpublished autobiography, 'the damage was more severe than usual, as this time it was obvious that the table upon which the bone lay had been subjected to what one might say was severe pressure for one of the legs was cracked. I just couldn't believe my eyes.'

Seton now resolved to burn the bone but his wife refused to even consider the idea. For some reason, she couldn't bear to be rid of the thing and her husband's repeated attempts to persuade her otherwise resulted in terrible rows between the two.

The press now became aware of the strange happenings in Learmonth Gardens and reporters from Scotland, England and America flocked to Edinburgh to cover the story. Seton found himself on the front page of several papers: 'they went to town with it, the whole story being magnified and I found myself again the leading figure in a story which I had begun to hate.'

One reporter from the Scottish Daily Mail borrowed the bone to get it photographed and was rushed into hospital with peritonitis after returning it. Another journalist borrowed it and was involved in a serious car accident. Coincidence, or was the bone responsible?

A few days before Christmas 1936, the Setons had yet another blazing row in front of their daughter's nanny which resulted in Zeyla and their daughter, Egidia, leaving for her parents. Seton left for his club but returned later that night to find the nanny in a terrible state. Around 6pm she had heard a terrible crash and the sound of breaking glass coming from the drawing room. Seton opened the door of the drawing room expecting to see the worst. He was surprised to see that all was in order except for the table on which the bone rested. It was overturned and broken, along with the display case. The bone had shattered into five pieces. A surgeon friend of Zeyda's was asked by her to repair it. He declared that on the first night it was in his possession a maid had seen a strange figure. She tried to run from it and had broken her leg.

The Christmas period saw the couple reunite but the disturbances continued. On Boxing Day, the bone became the topic of conversation during a dinner party:

> *Whilst we were talking a fresh round of drinks were being served. The entire table, Bone and all, went hurtling onto the wall opposite, with a terrific thump ... Chaos followed, the maid fainted, as did Zeyla's rather hysterical cousin Gert! The party became a fiasco from then on.*

Things now went from bad to worse with two mysterious fires breaking out in the house. The strange-looking figure was again seen. The Setons were also plagued by illness and Sir Alexander informed the press that his wife would now take the bone back to Egypt and restore it to the tomb in the hope that calm would be restored to their lives.

Seton was invited to speak at the Edinburgh Psychic College on 9 April 1937 where he spoke of the disturbances in his home. The bone was placed on a table in front of him. Mrs Boardman, a medium in attendance, warned Seton that he should get rid of the bone within six weeks. She saw the threat of blindness associated with any who touched the object if this was not done. She also spoke of a dark beckoning hand wearing a ring, the presence of which remained with her for several minutes. Seton remained open minded about the warning: 'I am absolutely and entirely open-minded. I refuse to be drawn into any controversy, because things have taken place which I cannot explain.'

The pledge to return the bone to the tomb remained unfulfilled, with Zeyla remaining strangely attached to the object despite all the apparent problems associated with it. Under no circumstances would she agree to it leaving her possession.

Scores of letters were sent to Learmonth Gardens about the bone, including one from Howard Carter, the discoverer of Tutankhamen's tomb. Despite being sceptical in public about the notion of Egyptian curses, Carter confided to Seton that, 'things quite inexplicable like this could happen, indeed had happened and will go on happening.'

Seton was now at breaking point and decided to destroy the bone. He called on his uncle, a priest from St Benedict's Abbey at Fort William, to visit the house. As Seton's daughter later recalled, 'He was in charge of wines and spirits up in the Abbey and I rather think he was their best customer. He came down and waved his hands over the bone a bit and incanted something. After the Drunken Monk had exorcised it, it was put in an incinerator and burnt.'

Zeyla was incensed on learning of the destruction of her treasured possession and the already shaky marriage finally collapsed. They were divorced in 1939. Both went on to remarry but any hope that the destruction of the bone would end the curse proved sadly futile. Ill-health, financial problems and sadness continued to plague them for the rest of their lives.

Seton died in 1963, the same year as his ex-wife. Sceptics were later to claim that the whole business had been invented so that Seton could sell the story to the newspapers – something which Sir Alexander always firmly denied. Others suggested that his wife had even faked some of the phenomena in order to provide her with an excuse to end the marriage.

Seton's daughter in later life continued to maintain that the bone was an object of evil. She even went as far as to claim that all who touched the bone had died before their time. The former nanny, interviewed some two years after her employer's death, also confirmed much of what Seton had said about the bone and the paranormal activity connected with it.

Reflecting on the matter some years before, Sir Alexander wrote how he could 'give no answer as to what caused these mysterious happenings, but to my mind there was some strange power released that we humans are apt to laugh at, but which was oh so very real! Looking back on this experience I still think it was one of the most horrible experiences that I have been through, happening as it did both in the daytime and the night. My own interpretation of the matter is that through some uncanny power of religion it was brought under destructive control. But if – and I emphasise the word 'if' – it really did carry a curse, as many people thought, the curse certainly did not end when I destroyed *the Bone* by fire, and from 1936 onwards trouble, sometimes grave, seemed to be always around the corner.'

Chapter 18

THE CROGLIN HORROR

The image of the vampire has been firmly entrenched in our collective consciousness for centuries. Indeed, the belief in blood sucking demons and spirits was widespread across many parts of southern and eastern Europe from at least medieval times.

Great Britain, on the other hand, can boast only a handful of such tales and one of these is even claimed to be a genuine account of a vampire attack that took place in a sleepy Cumberland hamlet in the latter half of Queen Victoria's reign!

The story first became widely known after it was published in 1896 by Augustus Hare, author and traveller, in a series of books entitled *The Story of my Life*. Hare claimed that he had first became aware of the vampire story during a dinner party held in June 1874. His informant was a certain Captain Fisher – Edward Fisher-Rowe – who was soon to marry a member of Hare's family, one Lady Victoria Liddel. The Fishers owned a single-storey building known as Croglin Grange in Cumberland. They decided to move to Thorncombe in Surrey (where Captain Fisher was born in 1832) and so rented their home to two brothers and a sister. It should be noted that Hare never once gives us the names of the tenants or even the precise date for the incident, although it is implied by later writers that it occurred in the 1870s.

To quote from Hare's book:

> *They were extremely fortunate in their tenants, two brothers and a sister. They heard their praises from all quarters. To their poorer neighbours they were all that is most kind and beneficent, and their neighbours of a higher class spoke of them as a most welcome addition to the little society of the neighbourhood. On their part the tenants were greatly delighted with their new residence. The arrangement of the house, which*

A *19ᵗʰ-century depiction of a vampire attack. (public domain)*

would have been a trial to many, was not so to them. In every respect Croglin Grange was exactly suited to them.

The winter was spent most happily by the new inmates of Croglin Grange, who shared in all the little social pleasures of the district, and made themselves very popular. In the following summer, there was one day which was dreadfully, annihilatingly hot. The brothers lay under the trees with their books, for it was too hot for any active occupation. The sister sat in the verandah and worked, or tried to work, for, in the intense sultriness of that summer day, work was next to impossible. They dined early, and after dinner they still sat out in the verandah, enjoying the cool air which came with evening, and they watched the sun set, and the moon rise over the belt of trees which separated the grounds from the churchyard, seeing it mount the heavens till the whole lawn was bathed in silver light, across which the long shadows from the shrubbery fell as if embossed, so vivid and distinct were they.

When they separated for the night, all retiring to their rooms on the ground floor (for, as I said, there was no upstairs in that house), the sister felt that the heat was still so great that she could not sleep, and having fastened her window, she did not close the shutters – in that very quiet place it was not necessary – and, propped against the pillows, she still watched the wonderful, the marvellous beauty of that summer night. Gradually she became aware of two lights, two lights which flickered in and out in the belt of trees which separated the lawn from the churchyard, and as her gaze became fixed upon them, she saw them emerge, fixed in a dark substance, a definite ghastly something, which seemed every moment to become nearer, increasing in size and substance as it approached. Every now and then it was lost for a moment in the long shadows which stretched across the lawn from the trees, and then it emerged larger than ever, and still coming on – on. As she watched it, the most uncontrollable horror seized her. She longed to get away, but the door was close to the window and the door was locked on the inside, and while she was unlocking it, she must be for an instant nearer to it. She longed to scream, but her voice seemed paralysed, her tongue glued to the roof of her mouth.

Suddenly, she never could explain why afterwards, the terrible object seemed to turn to one side, seemed to be going round the house, not to be coming to her at all, and immediately she jumped out of bed and rushed to the door, but as she was unlocking it, she heard scratch, scratch, scratch upon the window, and saw a hideous brown face with flaming eyes glaring in at her. She rushed back to the bed, but the creature continued to scratch, scratch, scratch upon the window. She felt a sort of mental comfort in the knowledge that the window was securely fastened on the inside. Suddenly the scratching sound ceased, and a kind of pecking sound took its place. Then, in her agony, she became aware that the creature was unpicking the lead! The noise continued, and a diamond pane of glass fell into the room. Then a long bony finger of the creature came in and turned the handle of the window, and the window opened, and the creature came in; and it came across the room, and her terror was so great that she could not scream, and it came up to the bed, and it twisted its long, bony fingers into her hair, and it dragged her head over the side of the bed, and – it bit her violently in the throat.

As it bit her, her voice was released, and she screamed with all her might and main. Her brothers rushed out of their rooms, but the door was locked on the inside. A moment was lost while they got a poker and broke it open. Then the creature had already escaped through the window, and the sister, bleeding violently from a wound in the throat, was lying unconscious over the side of the bed. One brother pursued the creature, which fled before him through the moonlight with gigantic strides, and eventually seemed to disappear over the wall into the churchyard. Then he rejoined his brother by the sister's bedside. She was dreadfully hurt and her wound was a very definite one, but she was of strong disposition, not given either to romance or superstition, and when she came to herself she said, 'What has happened is most extraordinary and I am very much hurt. It seems inexplicable, but of course there is an explanation, and we must wait for it. It will turn out that a lunatic has escaped from some asylum and found his way here.' The wound healed and she appeared to get well, but the doctor who was sent for would not believe that she could bear so terrible a shock so easily, and insisted that she must have change, mental and physical; so her brothers took her to Switzerland.

Being a sensible girl, when she went abroad, she threw herself at once into the interests of the country she was in. She dried plants, she made sketches, she went up mountains, and, as autumn came on, she was the person who urged that they should return to Croglin Grange. 'We have taken it,' she said, 'for seven years, and we have only been there once; and we shall always find it difficult to let a house which is only one storey high, so we had better return there; lunatics do not escape every day.' As she urged it, her brothers wished nothing better, and the family returned to Cumberland. From there being no upstairs in the house, it was impossible to make any great change in their arrangements. The sister occupied the same room, but it is unnecessary to say she always closed her shutters, which, however, as in many old houses, always left one top pane of the window uncovered. The brothers moved, and occupied a room together exactly opposite that of their sister, and they always kept loaded pistols in their room.

The winter passed most peacefully and happily. In the following March the sister was suddenly awakened by a sound she remembered only too well – scratch, scratch, scratch upon the window, and looking up, she saw, climbed up to the topmost pane of the window, the same hideous brown shrivelled face, with glaring eyes, looking in at her. This time she screamed as loud as she could. Her brothers rushed out of their room with pistols, and out of the front door. The creature was already scudding away across the lawn. One of the brothers fired and hit it in the leg, but still with the other leg it continued to make way, scrambled over the wall into the churchyard, and seemed to disappear into a vault which belonged to a family long extinct.

The next day the brothers summoned all the tenants of Croglin Grange, and in their presence the vault was opened. A horrible scene revealed itself. The vault was full of coffins; they had been broken open, and their contents, horribly mangled and distorted, were scattered over the floor. One coffin alone remained intact. Of that the lid had been lifted, but still lay loose upon the coffin. They raised it, and there, brown, withered, shrivelled, mummified, but quite entire, was the same hideous figure which had looked in at the windows of Croglin Grange, with the marks of a recent pistol-shot in the leg; and they did the only thing that can lay a vampire – they burnt it.

And so ends the account.

Over the years, the story has been repeated in many books and articles on the paranormal and several of these contain new alleged 'facts' on the case:

- *The names of the two brothers and sister are given as Michael, Edward and Amelia Cranswell.*
- *The events took place between 1873 and 1876. This is despite the fact that Hare mentions it in an entry dated June 1874!*
- *The vault belonged to the Fisher family.*
- *A three-year-old child was also attacked but the parents attributed the marks on her neck to rats.*
- *The pistols and lead were purchased in Switzerland. The coloured lead used in the shot enabled the brothers to easily identify the vampire upon searching the vault.*
- *A certain Jem Crosswell, gamekeeper, helped the brothers search the vault.*
- *The body in the coffin was wearing a long cloak.*
- *A stake was driven through the vampire's heart.*

Some of this information was based on local oral history and was repeated to F. Clive-Ross, a writer who visited the area in the early 60s. However, it is also fair to say that a great deal of the other 'facts' owe perhaps more to the imagination of Valentine Dyall – actor, radio presenter and author – who wrote twice about the story in a 1954 issue of *Fate* magazine and in his book, *Unsolved Mysteries*, also published in 1954.

It was Dyall who first gave us the names of the tenants and the gamekeeper. The same goes for the stake in the vampire's heart and the Swiss ammunition. We do not know if Dyall visited the area but Clive-Ross was told that the Cranswells were remembered locally. In light of this, can we assume that Dyall received his information from local sources? Or did his version of the tale simply taint certain aspects of the case locally in the years following the publication of his own account of the vampire?

The Croglin incident is now regarded by some paranormal researchers as a classic example of real life vampirism. Indeed, dip into many book on the subject and you can usually find an account of Croglin Grange.

So what is the truth behind Hare's account? Was it a massive leg-pull on his or Fisher's part, a tale designed to titillate Victorian readers with tales of violence and sexual undertones?

Charles G. Harper certainly thought so. In his book *Haunted Houses*, published in 1907, it was pointed out that there was no such place as Croglin Grange. However, he noted that there were two farm houses known as Croglin High Hall and Croglin Low Hall. Neither building had a single storey, nor was there a nearby church. Indeed, the nearest church was roughly two miles away. So on the surface it does appear that Hare's story is a work of fiction ... or was it?

Local gossip does indeed refer to a vampire legend and points to Croglin Low Hall as the scene of the horror. There is even a blocked up window on the ground floor which has been long pointed out to researchers as the window where the 'vampire' attacked Amelia. There is also structural evidence to suggest that the building once possessed a single storey – a stone support for a roof beam can be seen in the ground floor room where Amelia was said to have slept. According to local tradition, the property received a second storey in the 1720s – thereby placing the story further back than the 1870s. There was even a nearby church, with a burial vault, which had been damaged during the English Civil War and was later demolished in the late 17th and or early 18th century. Traces of it could be

CROGLIN LOW HALL.

Croglin Low Hall – scene of the alledged vampire attack. (public domain)

seen as late as the 1930s in the form of ploughed up stones in a field known as Church Field. Also, the house had been known as Croglin Grange until at least the 1720s and had once been occupied by the Fisher family.

Clive-Ross even found a Mrs Dorothy Parkin, whose husband, Inglewood Parkin, had owned the estate on which Croglin Low Hall stood:

Mrs Parkin tells me that she spoke with one of the Fisher family, who was born in the middle- 1860s, and that he told her he had known the vampire tale all his life, and originally heard it from his grandparents.

Local folk memory places the story in the aftermath of the English Civil War with dates ranging from the 1650s to the 1690s. The addition of a second storey to Croglin and the removal of the church and burial vault by the 1720s also point to a date earlier than the Victorian period. So did Hare mishear Fisher's account as to the exact date and assumed that he was referring to himself rather than an ancestor? Or did Hare simply move the story to his own time for extra shock value?

But did Augustus Hare even imply the 1870s? Here is the original introduction to the story in Hare's book:

Captain Fisher also told us this really extraordinary story connected with his own family:

Fisher may sound a very plebeian name, but this family is of very ancient lineage, and for many hundreds of years they have possessed a very curious old place in Cumberland, which bears the weird name of Croglin Grange. The great characteristic of the house is that never at any period of its very long existence has it been more than one-storey high, but it has a terrace from which large grounds sweep away towards the church in the hollow, and a fine distant view.

When, in lapse of years, the Fishers outgrew Croglin Grange in family and fortune, they were wise enough not to destroy the long-standing characteristic of the place by adding another storey to the house, but they went away to the south, to reside at Thorncombe near Guildford, and they let Croglin Grange.

Fisher's retelling of his tale to Hare is dated 24 June 1874. However, at no point does Hare or Fisher actually say when the vampire attack is said to have taken place. I find it inconceivable that the newspapers would have failed to cover the story if it had occurred in the 1870s – although I am open to the possibility that the story was deliberately kept from the press in order to prevent a frenzy of media activity. But surely the police would have been called in when Ameila was first attacked by the creature? And yet not a single police record of the time makes any mention of it.

So we are back to local folklore and a date ranging from the late 17th to early 18th century.

It may surprise and disappoint some readers to learn that the Fishers did not own or even live at Croglin Low Hall in the 17th century (despite Fisher stating that his family had owned the building for hundreds of years). Local records show that a certain George Towry was in residence there in 1688, the previous owners having been the Howards and before them the Dacres. In 1727, the property was sold to a Mr Johnson. The Fishers only moved there in 1809 when an Edward Fisher is recorded as holding the lease. He died in 1833 and his tomb can be seen in Ainstable churchyard, which lies a mile or so from Croglin.

It appears that the Fishers only heard about the legend of the vampire from the previous occupants or their neighbours. By mistake or design, Captain Fisher attributed the story to his own family.

So what of the Croglin Vampire? Is the story fact or fiction?

I was originally inclined to dismiss the whole story as nonsense, especially after learning that the Fishers could not have occupied the hall when local tradition claims the alleged vampire attack took place. However, I have found that many folk tales and legends do often have an element of truth in them. I cannot help thinking that something occurred at Croglin during Towry's ownership of the Grange, something so shocking that it was remembered by later generations.

It should be noted that mental illness was little understood in the 17th century and was often attributed to the work of evil spirits, witchcraft or even the devil himself. Could it be that a vagrant was hiding in the area and using the ruined church and burial vault as a bolt hole? Did he only emerge at night in order to escape detection? Were his attacks sexually motivated and did the emaciated figure, after being shot, retreat to the vault where he died of shock due to loss of blood?

Imagine the horror of those who eventually found his corpse in the bone-strewn vault. In those superstitious times, it was hardly surprising that the whole incident was put down to the work of evil forces. With the popularity of vampire stories such as Varney the Vampire and Dracula in the 19th century, it was little wonder that later generations attributed the attacks to a vampire.

Chapter 19

THE BEAST OF MERIONETHSHIRE

In the 1880s an Oxford professor was holidaying with his wife and a friend in a cottage on the shores of a small mountain lake in the ancient county of Merionethshire in Wales.

One day, the professor was fly fishing a few yards from the shore when he stubbed his toe on something. He bent down and lifted up a strange looking skull. It appeared to be of a dog but was much broader in the head than any normal sized canine. The relic intrigued him and he decided to keep it as a souvenir, placing it on the kitchen shelf of their holiday home.

That evening, the professor and his friend decided to go for a walk, leaving the wife alone in the cottage. It was not long after their departure that she heard strange noises coming from the kitchen door.

She went to investigate and could clearly hear something that was trying to gain entry. The scratches and heavy breathing made her think that a dog from one of the nearby farms had been attracted by the light from their cottage. Suddenly, two massive paws appeared at the window. The lamp only heightened the horror as the dim light revealed through the diamond panes of glass the hideous jaw and red eyes of a creature that appeared a strange mixture of human and wolf.

The animal then vanished from the window and the terrified woman heard it circling the building. The realisation suddenly dawned on her that the front door had been left unlocked. She rushed to it and managed to close it just before the thing could reach it.

Seconds later she heard scratching, panting and snarling at the now-bolted door. Her terror lasted for untold minutes, with the animal ceaselessly pacing the cottage, seemingly still intent on finding a way in.

Medieval woodcut of a werewolf. (public domain)

Her fear was heightened by the knowledge that her husband and their guest would soon be back. They were both unarmed and would prove easy prey to the creature if it decided to attack them.

It was then that she heard voices in the garden and realised that the men were returning. She rushed to the door where she collapsed at her husband's feet in a state of shock. She was carried to the sofa where she managed to blurt out her story to the astonished pair.

The professor managed to calm her down and suggested that she retire to bed. He then decided with his companion to await the creature's possible return.

It was early morning when they both heard the footsteps of an animal approaching the building. The creature circled the cottage before jumping up at the kitchen window, scratching at the glass with its claws. Both men were shocked to see inches from them the luminous face of a wolf-like creature. It gazed at them for a few seconds before running from the window as the men rushed to give chase, arming themselves with a shotgun in case the creature turned to attack.

A shadowy shape was seen to run through the gate towards the lake where it scampered across the shingle and into the water. Not even a ripple marked its sudden disappearance.

The professor became convinced that the skull was somehow connected with the creature and in the morning took the thing from the kitchen and flung it back into the lake. The 'wolf-man' was never seen again.

So what had terrorised the professor, his wife and their friend that night? Was the discovery of the skull just a coincidence and had the creature simply been a large and fearsome dog as some have suggested? I have an open mind but it is interesting to note that early 19th-century folk-tales from the area do tell of a 'man-wolf' roaming the hills and paths, a thing that had terrified the shepherds and their flocks.

And what of the following Merionethshire story? It may be a coincidence but it also concerns an encounter with something that bears an uncanny resemblance to the creature in the first story. No date is given for the incident but my research would suggest that it took place in the late 19th or early 20th century.

A certain Miss St Denis was staying at a farm in Merionethshire. The building lay near a village, a small railway station and several disused slate quarries. The lady was an amateur artist and would often paint on the station platform as the surrounding views from there were particularly striking. On one occasion, she had stayed painting later than usual when she noticed the figure of a man sitting on one of the nearby railway trucks. He was staring at her intently. She felt surprise at this as the station was hardly used. Indeed, this was the first time that she had seen another soul there in the evening apart from the station master. The station master had already left for home and so could not be him.

She began to feel uneasy as the man continued to stare at her. She deliberately coughed but he did not react. A second cough also failed to bring any reaction. She then called out, 'Can you tell me the time, please?' but the figure still did not respond.

She then decided to pack her things and made her way out of the station. She glanced back and was horrified to see that the man was now following her. She quickened her pace and started to whistle in order to appear unconcerned. It was now twilight and the path had taken her to a remote spot surrounded by cliffs and disused quarries. The lady realised that a cry for help out here would go unheard and so she decided to confront her stalker. She spun round and shouted, 'What do you want? How dare you!'

The man did not respond. She was now able to see him clearly as the last rays of sunlight fell on the path as he drew near. He was not a man after all. The thing appeared to be covered in grey hair and, although human in form, had a wolf's head. It sprang forward with a look of ferocity on its face. The terrified woman quickly grabbed a torch from her pocket and shone it at the beast. The thing shrank back, its paws trying to hide the light from its face. It then faded away leaving her alone in the darkness.

The lady was shaken but unhurt. The next day she decided to make enquiries in the area to see if she could discover any reason for what she had seen. She learnt that some bones, a mixture of human and animal, had been found in a slate quarry close to where the apparition had vanished. It emerged that the quarry had a bad reputation and was shunned by locals after dusk. She could learn nothing more. She later told her story to Elliott O'Donnell, the author of many books on the supernatural. He decided to publish her encounter in his 1912 book *Werewolves*.

Go to Merionethshire today and you may yet hear folk-tales of ghostly wolf-like creatures being seen at dusk on the hills and paths. Of course, you could dismiss such stories as nothing more than local gossip and leg pulling. But would you really want to take a chance and walk the lonely and forbidding hills as the sun sets?

Chapter 20

THE PSYCHIC LEGACY OF JACK THE RIPPER

Jack the Ripper is the most famous serial killer in history. He murdered at least five women in Whitechapel between August and November 1888 before disappearing as mysteriously as he had arrived. To this day, debate still rages as to his motives and identity – suspects include a member of the British Royal Family, an Irish-American quack doctor, a Liverpool cotton merchant, a barrister and even the author of Alice in Wonderland!

It is little wonder that some believe his horrific crimes have psychically tainted the streets and buildings of the East End. I have spoken to many East Enders who believe that the ghosts of his victims – and even the Ripper himself – still linger in the alleyways of Whitechapel.

Mary Ann 'Polly' Nichols

'Polly' Nichols was found on Buck's Row – later renamed Durward Street – in the early hours of 31 August. She is generally regarded as the Ripper's first victim. Her throat had been cut and she displayed abdominal mutilations. For many years afterwards, locals claimed that a huddled-up figure in shabby Victorian clothes, emitting a ghostly light, was sometimes seen lying in the gutter. Horses would often panic upon reaching the spot where 'Polly' had died. Dogs also reacted badly when passing there and would strain at the leash to avoid walking over the site of her murder.

Annie Chapman

Annie Chapman was murdered in the yard of 29 Hanbury Street on 8 September. Her head had almost been severed from her body and the mutilations were even more horrific than the previous victim. The Ripper had

The murder of Annie Chapman as reported by The Illustrated Police News. (Stewart Evans)

even removed her uterus. The area soon gained a reputation of being haunted with screams, moans and running footsteps being heard at night. Some even claimed to have seen a headless figure sitting on a wall in the yard.

A man named Thomas lived in the street and had been passing the scene of the murder one night in the 1920s when he heard the sounds of a struggle, muffled voices and panting coming from the doorway that led to the yard. Thinking that someone was being attacked, he walked through the passageway and found himself standing before the very spot where Annie Chapman had been murdered some 40 years before. The yard was deserted but he could still hear the sounds and they appeared to come from just below the step before him. The sounds of heavy breathing and gasping suddenly stopped and this was replaced by a dragging or swishing noise which also appeared to emanate from the same area. The sounds then ceased. Thomas waited a few moments but nothing else occurred. He then left the yard. He later learned that others had also heard the noises of a struggle coming from the murder site.

Figures were also seen in the area. In the 1920s a Mr Chapman – no relation to the victim – lived directly opposite number 29. He often observed two people entering the doorway that led to the yard. They were usually seen early in the morning and most often in the autumn. The witness was an early riser due to work and had opened his bedroom curtains when he first saw a couple vanish into the doorway opposite. He noticed that the woman was wearing a long skirt and appeared elderly. The man was immediately behind her and was wearing a greatcoat and a tall hat with a wide brim.

His next sighting of the couple was in the street itself. He was leaving early for work when he saw a man and woman walking towards him on the other side of the street. Upon reaching 29 Hanbury Street, they again disappeared into the doorway which led to the backyard. The couple appeared to be dressed as before. It was raining and he thought it odd that he had not heard any sounds from them, not even footsteps.

A couple of months were to pass before Mr Chapman saw them again from his bedroom window. They were again approaching number 29 and he called his wife to look. She jumped out of bed but was too late to see them enter the doorway. She did notice that both doors leading into the yard and house were closed. She was puzzled as to why she had not seen the door closing behind them. It was then that Mr Chapman realised that he had not seen the door open – the couple had appeared to melt into the door itself.

Mr Chapman made enquiries about the couple but no one could offer any explanation as to their identity. Several years then passed and he had all but forgotten about them.

Mr Chapman's brother had moved in with him and his wife after becoming a widower. They both worked for the same company and sometimes shared the same early-morning shift. One morning they left early and were walking towards Wilkes Street. Mr Chapman was amazed to see the same couple walking on the other side of the street. Both were talking, the man being just in front of the woman who was being forced to walk close to the wall. Mr Chapman nudged his brother, jerking his head towards the couple as they walked towards number 29. He then stopped his brother and they both turned round – the couple had vanished. Chapman said, 'There, you saw them, who on earth are they? His brother replied, 'Saw who? I didn't see anyone … I thought I heard the sound of footsteps on the other side of the road and I thought that's what you were trying to tell me.'

That was the last occasion that Chapman saw the mysterious couple. He later discovered that a rag and bone man had also seen the pair enter

number 29 but had thought nothing of it. Chapman became convinced that he had seen the ghost of Annie Chapman and her killer.

Elliott O'Donnell, the noted ghost hunter, had investigated this haunting and had found that sightings of the couple had started to circulate just after the murder. Their last reported appearance was around 1930. He believed that violent events often left a psychic

The yard at 29 Hanbury Street – scene of Annie Chapman's murder. (Stewart Evans)

residue which gradually faded away after a period of 50 years. He was convinced that the ghosts of Annie Chapman and Jack the Ripper had been created by the strong negative emotions generated on that fateful September morning in 1888.

Number 29 was demolished in 1970 and a brewery built on the site. It was noted that a chill was often felt in the boardroom at 6am on the anniversary of the murder. A figure of a woman was also seen by a wall in the storeroom. It was surmised that this figure was Annie Chapman.

Annie is also said to haunt the Ten Bells pub where she used to drink. Indeed, she was said to have been seen drinking in the pub just hours before her murder. Gusts of wind and poltergeist activity, such as objects being moved, have been attributed to her. Another victim of the Ripper – Mary Kelly – also used the pub and some have suggested that the activity witnessed there is actually down to her.

Windsor Barracks is also another alleged haunt of Annie Chapman. The figure of a woman sitting on a wall near the barracks is said to be her, the sole basis for this belief being that she lived in Windsor in the 1880s.

Elizabeth Stride

Elizabeth Stride was found in the yard of a working men's club in Berner Street – now Henriques Street – on 30 September. Her throat had been cut but there were no other mutilations. It is theorised that the Ripper had been disturbed by an approaching horse and cart and had fled the scene. Others believe that her murder had no connection with the Ripper. It has been suggested that she was a victim

Elliott O'Donnell was the first author to write of supernatural events connected with the murder sites in Whitechapel. (public domain)

of domestic dispute and that her death on the same night as Catherine Eddowes was simply a coincidence.

Elliott O'Donnell records that about a month after the murder, a tradesman was walking through Berner Street, heading for Commercial Road, when he heard a series of moans and groans. A small crowd soon gathered but no one could pin-point where the sounds were coming from. The tradesman was about to knock on one of the doors when a local woman in the crowd called out, 'It's no good knocking there, guv'nor. Them sounds don't come from that 'ouse. They're in the street 'ere. We've often 'eard them since poor Lizzie Stride was done to death.'

Catherine Eddowes

Catherine Eddowes died on the very same night as Elizabeth Stride. Her body was found in Mitre Square. Her throat had been cut, her body mutilated and the uterus and left kidney removed.

A Ripper suspect is seen taking to Catherine Eddowes. (Stewart Evans)

The murders of Stride and Eddowes as covered by The Illustrated Police News. (Stewart Evans)

The spot where Catherine died acquired the name 'Ripper's Corner' and it was said that her ghost could be seen there in late September or on the very anniversary of her murder. Elliott O'Donnell records that witnesses of her ghostly form included a policeman, a doctor and even a member of O'Donnell's own family. The late Peter Underwood, author and former president of the Ghost Club, was told by a medical student about the time he had crossed the square one late September night. He saw what he assumed was a bundle of clothes but then noticed that it appeared to move. Rushing over to help, he noticed that it was a woman lying on her back, her arms spread out from her body and her feet lying towards the gutter. She appeared to be in her 40s and was wearing a light dress under a coat. He was about 15 feet from her when she suddenly vanished. He had not taken his eyes off her and so ruled out the possibility that she had got up and fled.

A young couple decided to visit Mitre Square one Saturday evening after hearing about one of the Ripper's victims being found there. They entered the square and noticed a man hurrying away in the opposite direction. They then saw a bundle of clothing in one corner and assumed it was rubbish. Walking towards it they then realised that it was actually the body of a woman. She appeared quite still and the square suddenly became strangely quiet. They were about to approach the body when they heard voices and a group of five or six youths ran into the square. They decided to leave but upon looking back noticed that the figure of the woman had vanished – the youths were playing around at the very spot where they had seen the figure of the woman!

A legend is also linked to Mitre Square. This concerns the Priory of the Holy Trinity which stood on the site. In 1530 a monk called Brother Martin went mad and murdered a woman after seeing her at prayer before the altar. He then killed himself. The area became unhallowed ground and it was claimed in one publication of the time that the murder of Eddowes was actually committed at the behest of the phantom monk.

Mary Jane Kelly

Mary Kelly was murdered on 9 November 1888. She is thought to be the Ripper's last victim and the only one to be killed indoors. She had been horribly mutilated and her heart was absent. It was surmised that the killer had taken it with him.

The room at 13 Miller's Court, Dorset Street, was reputed to be haunted in the years following her death. A figure in black was seen to enter the room and then gaze out through the window. Locals believed it to be the ghost of Mary. The room also possessed a bloody hand-print on the wall. No matter how many times it was painted over it always showed through. A picture of the Crucifixion was finally used to hide it. 13 Miller's Court was finally demolished in the late 1920s. The ghostly figure of a woman continued to be seen in the building which later occupied the site.

Two people claimed to have seen Mary Kelly immediately after her death. One, Caroline Maxwell, a witness at the inquest and acquaintance of Kelly's, said she had spoken to her at around 8.30am, several hours after the time given by the coroner as the time of Kelly's death. Kelly said she had 'the horrors of drink'

Mary Kelly in Miller's Court. (Stewart Evans)

Mary Kelly with Jack the Ripper. (Stewart Evans)

upon her and was urged by Mrs Maxwell to take another drink to steady herself. Kelly replied that she had and vomited it up. About an hour later, she saw Kelly again, this time talking to a stout man in dark clothes outside the Britannia pub. She described her appearance in some detail, and was sure that she was not mistaken about the date. Another, Maurice Lewis, a tailor who lived in Dorset Street, said that he saw Kelly drinking in the Britannia pub. This would have been around 10am. He had also seen her at 8am in the street. Like Maxwell, these sightings were actually made several hours after her death. He was certain that it was her as he had known Kelly for five years. Some paranormal researchers have suggested that they both unwittingly saw Mary Kelly's ghost.

Mary was buried in St Patrick's Roman Catholic Cemetery at Leytonstone on 19 November 1888. Some visitors to her grave have claimed to have felt her presence there.

The Illustrated Police News covered the Ripper murders extensively. (Stewart Evans)

Westminster Bridge

On 31 December a figure is said to appear on the east side of the bridge. As Big Ben chimes midnight the apparition leaps into the cold waters of the Thames. Legend states that this is the ghost of Jack the Ripper. He supposedly threw himself from the bridge in 1888 in order to escape the hangman's noose after the murder of Mary Kelly and is now doomed to re-enact his last moments for eternity. This apparition is linked by some to Montague John Druitt, a school master and barrister, who committed suicide by throwing himself in the Thames in December 1888. Druitt was named as a suspect by Chief Constable Sir Melville Macnaghten in a private memorandum written in 1894. Macnaghten claimed to possess 'private information' that left 'little doubt' Druitt's own family thought he was Jack the Ripper. However, Druitt killed himself further upstream at Chiswick and so cannot be the phantom seen on Westminster Bridge.

So is Whitechapel still haunted by the Ripper and his victims? The area has undergone major redevelopment since the Second World War and the murder sites have changed almost beyond all recognition. In light of this, you would think that all psychic traces of the Ripper and his victims would have long since been erased by the demolition gangs and new building developments. And yet some visitors to Whitechapel still claim to sense both the presence of the Ripper and his victims in some of the streets and alleys – especially Mitre Square. Some East Enders continue to make a conscious effort to avoid the crime scenes after dark, claiming that gasps, muffled cries and running footsteps are still occasionally heard there.

One thing is for certain, Jack the Ripper, the terrible fate of his victims and the mystery of his identity will continue to fascinate and horrify people for centuries to come.

RECOMMENDED READING

Chapter One – The Naked Embrace
The Restless Spirits of Langenhoe (2000) John C. Dening
A Host of Hauntings (1973) Peter Underwood

Chapter Two – The Gladwish Terror
Adventures with Phantoms (1946) R. Thurston Hopkins
The Ghost Hunters (1985) Peter Underwood

Chapter Three – The Enigma of the Hexham Heads
Quest for the Hexham Heads (2010) Paul Screeton

Chapter Four – The Treasurer's House
Haunted York (2009) Rupert Matthews

Chapter Five – The Grey Man of Ben MacDhui
The Big Grey Man of Ben Macdhui (1970) Affleck Gray

Chapter Six – The Curse of William Corder's Skull
Ghosts Over England (1953) R. Thurston Hopkins
Haunted Bury St Edmunds (2006) Alan Murdie

Chapter Seven – Ghosts of the Bloody Tower
Haunted London (1973) Peter Underwood

Chapter Eight – The Hairy Hands of Dartmoor
The Witchcraft and Folklore of Dartmoor (1965) Ruth E. St. Leger-Gordon

Chapter Nine – The Monks of St Dunstan's
No Common Task (1983) Peter Underwood

Chapter Ten – The Green Lady of Fyvie Castle and Other Haunting Tales
The Curse of Fyvie Castle. The Unexplained magazine series (1980-1983)
   Pages 2,850 -2,853. Frank Smyth

Chapter Eleven – Shadows of Evil
Ghost Writer (1966) Fred Archer
A Ghost Hunter's Game Book (1958) James Wentworth Day
Ghosts Over Britain (1977) Peter Moss

Chapter Twelve – The Crawling Lady of Ardachie
To Catch the Moon from the Bottom of the Sea (2009) Peter McEwan
Worlds Beyond (1986) Ian Wilson

Chapter Thirteen – The Agony of Marie le Moyne
Haunted Royal Homes (1987) Joan Forman

Chapter Fourteen – Ealing's House of Death
Our Haunted Kingdom (1973) Andrew Green

Chapter Fifteen – The Lady and the Butterfly
Haunted Bath (2009) David Brandon

Chapter Sixteen – Beyond Harry Price – The Ghosts of Borley Church
The Borley Rectory Companion (2018) Paul Adams, Eddie Brazil and Peter Underwood
The Ghosts of Borley (1973) Paul Tabori & Peter Underwood

Chapter Seventeen – The Curse of the Setons
The Transgressions of a Baronet (unpublished autobiography) Sir Alexander Hay Seton

Chapter Eighteen – The Croglin Horror
Haunted Churches & Abbeys of Britain (1978) Marc Alexander
Unsolved Mysteries (1954) Valentine Dyall
Tomorrow Vol. XI No. II (Spring 1963) F. Clive-Ross.
The Story of My Life (1896) Augustus Hare

Chapter Nineteen – The Beast of Merionethshire
50 Great Horror Stories (1969) Edited by John Canning
Werewolves (1912) Elliott O'Donnell

Chapter Twenty – The Psychic legacy of Jack the Ripper

Jack the Ripper: Letters from Hell (2005) Stewart P. Evans & Keith Skinner

Jack the Ripper: Scotland Yard Investigates (2006) Stewart P. Evans & Donald Rumblelow

The Ultimate Jack the Ripper Sourcebook (2002) Stewart P. Evans & Keith Skinner

Jack the Ripper: 100 Years of Mystery (1987) Peter Underwood

Further Reading

Phantom Britain (1975) Marc Alexander

A Natural History of Ghosts (2013) Roger Clarke

Haunted Britain (1973) Anthony D. Hippisley Coxe

In Search of Ghosts (1969) James Wentworth Day

Cavalcade of Ghosts (1956) R. Thurston Hopkins

Haunted Britain (1948) Elliott O'Donnell

Trees of Ghostly Dread (1958) Elliott O'Donnell

The Haunted Realm (1986) Simon Marsden

Phantoms of the Isles (1990) Simon Marsden

The Journal of a Ghost Hunter (1994) Simon Marsden

This Spectred Isle (Revised edition, 2005) Simon Marsden

Phantom Footsteps (1959) Alisdair Alpin MacGregor

Supernatural England (2002) Betty Puttick

The A-Z of British Ghosts (1992) Peter Underwood

About the Author

John West was born in London. He first became interested in ghosts as a child when he discovered his mother's collection of paperbacks on the supernatural. He was immediately drawn to the strange cover illustrations of phantom ladies, ruined castles and sinister shadows and was doubly spellbound by the frightening stories contained within. Over the next few years, John devoured every book on ghosts that he could find and this, in turn, led to him visiting many alleged haunted places across the UK.

John's fascination with the supernatural has never left him and now, some 40 years later, he finds himself writing about ghosts for *Psychic News* magazine as well as appearing on radio and TV to talk about Britain's ghostly inhabitants. And has he ever seen a ghost? The answer is no but he has had some strange experiences over the years. In Borley churchyard, his mobile phone went haywire and took over 40 photos in rapid succession – all of which were blank. Another time, he heard a large dog running up the stairs of a former home in Lincolnshire. His dog, Lucky, was fast asleep on the bed at the time!

John is the author of several books and many articles on non-ghostly subjects ranging from the Romans and Victorian murders to celebrity interviews. He has been interviewed on BBC and independent radio about ghosts and folklore and hosts a radio show in Norfolk which is ghost-free. He was also the regular guest historian on Mustard TV in Norfolk – a station now sadly closed.

John is also a film producer – alongside director Jason Figgis – and has several film credits to his name, including a feature-length documentary on the photographer and ghost enthusiast Sir Simon Marsden, which features narration by the late Sir John Hurt. He dabbles in acting too and has appeared as a supporting artist in The Detectorists, The Crown and The Personal History of David Copperfield. He also plays one of the leads in Winifred Meeks, a haunted house film by Jason Figgis ... and yes – as you would expect – John lives in a haunted house in Suffolk!

Printed in Great Britain
by Amazon

59583895R00111